THE READING LIST:
Literature, love and back again

by Leslie Shimotakahara

Published in 2011 by Stories That Bind
STB is an imprint of Variety Crossing Press

Released 2012

Library and Archives Canada Cataloguing in Publication

Shimotakahara, Leslie
The reading list / Leslie Shimotakahara.

Includes bibliographical references.
ISBN 978-0-9812279-3-1

1. Shimotakahara, Leslie.
2. Authors, Canadian (English)--21st
century--Biography. I. Title.

PS8637.H525Z47 2011   C818'.603   C2010-907164-6

Publisher: Dae-Tong Huh
Managing Editor: Sandra Huh
Copy Editor: Martha Uniacke Breen
Design and Layout: Sandra Huh
Cover Design: Natalia Reis Designs
Author Photo: Christos Grivas

stb
STORIES THAT BIND

is an imprint of Variety Crossing Press.
PO Box 45035 5854 Yonge St.
Willowdale, ON, M2M 4K3, Canada
Phone: 416-912-6466
E-mail: varietycrossing@gmail.com
Web site: www.varietycrossing.org

For my family

You have all heard of people whom the loss of their books has turned into invalids, or of those who in order to acquire them became criminals.

-Walter Benjamin, "Unpacking My Library"

TABLE OF CONTENTS

Author's Note:

The Reading List is a work of literary non-fiction. To acknowledge the literary aspect of my writing and respect the privacy of certain individuals (who might otherwise disown me), I have used fictitious names in some instances, and collapsed chronologies and events for narrative purposes.

THE READING LIST:
Literature, love and back again

chapter one

The works of the great poets have never yet been read by mankind, for only great poets can read them.

-Henry David Thoreau, *Walden*

My father had never read a novel in his life, but he liked that I was an English professor. At the supermarket, at the drycleaner, in line at Coffee Time – he somehow managed to work it into small talk with strangers. When I'd first completed my Ph.D., his pride was touching, and I recalled feeling a surge of satisfaction upon seeing that on my graduation card, he'd drawn a crown beside "To Dr. Leslie." After retiring, he'd even expressed an interest in taking up reading and asked me to put together a list of "greatest hits" – of course, I'd never gotten around to it.

"So what are you teaching these days?" His voiced opened up like a kid at a museum.

"Right now, I'm not teaching much of anything." It was the end of the semester, and I was up to my eyeballs in marking.

Through the static of my cell phone, I heard him padding to the fridge and opening a can of pop. "You must be giving exams?"

"Right."

"It must be fun to read the ideas of bright young minds and see how your lectures have shaped them."

I cringed at the note of enchantment in his voice. It was all too reminiscent of the wonder I'd felt not so long ago at the mere mention of higher education. But that was before I'd actually become a professor. That was before I'd endured the blinding lights of the lecture hall, my pulse hammering so hard I could barely read my own notes, or was it the downpour of sweat in my eyes that was making it difficult to see anything? The worst part was always the students' expectant stares. Even as I stood there stammering and spewing gibberish, they looked at me with full confidence that I knew my stuff – even if they didn't much like me. So I was forced to act the role of the eccentric, erudite scholar, puffing out my chest and making ridiculous hand gestures as I tried to explain the most complicated ideas, all the while affecting a snobbish air of this-stuff-is-way-above-your-heads-anyway. Not surprisingly, the kids zoned out; and come paper time, they just googled "Henry James" and went on Wikipedia.

But Daddy thought I loved being a professor, and who was I to shatter his illusions?

"Teaching's all right, but it's not my real passion. Research is what I live for."

It's what all academics are trained to say during grad school, and the higher up the pecking order your university, the more you're encouraged to thumb your nose. "Why would I want to waste my time teaching?" said my friend at Harvard, before jumping on a plane for Italy. To say you like teaching is all but admitting that you haven't published squat and can't get a research grant to save your life.

But I'd found myself wondering lately: how much did I truly love the research? Years ago, as a bright-eyed grad student, I had been thrilled to be initiated into the world of "isms" (modernism, post-modernism, post-colonialism, post-structuralism, new criticism, new historicism, new formalism, and more new "isms" are probably being coined as we speak). At first, it had been a joy to throw around these terms in seminars and at conferences; none of us quite had any idea what we were talking about, but who the hell cared? It was intoxicating to feel we'd arrived at the academic hothouse. We were the new new intelligentsia.

At some point between third and fourth year, however, all the posturing started to seem a tad sophomoric. It was irritating to be surrounded by colleagues who threw around these empty theoretical words, and it was even more irritating to be compelled to do the same, simply to prove I could hold my own.

When my dad asked what I was researching, my cheeks flushed and I choked on a cough. "Oh, it's *way* too complicated to explain. It wouldn't interest you anyway."

The truth was that I'd been immersed in the world of literary and cultural theory for so long that, to someone not in my field, I couldn't explain my way out of a paper bag. It was as impossible to communicate what I was working on to a layperson as it would be for anyone else to explain the meaning of "red" and "rock."

But it depressed me to think that I could no longer even have a normal conversation with my own father. A screw tightened in my chest and we lapsed into silence.

Daddy couldn't have sounded more cheerful. "By the way, congratulations on finishing your first year at St. Francis Xavier. Soon you'll be publishing books and jet-setting around the world. Appearing on talk shows."

My eyes stung. He had the strangest misconceptions about the life of a small-town professor.

The weeks of sleep deprivation had accumulated into a fuzzy layer wrapped around my head, and sharp tingles were shooting up my wrists constantly. I couldn't wait to give my last exam the next day and then sink into a scalding bath with a glass of icy vodka.

"So do you think you'll have time to visit Toronto over the summer?"

"I don't know." It hadn't even crossed my mind. Who had time for visiting anyone? I had bigger fish to fry, such as moving away from this godforsaken town out in the boondocks of Nova Scotia. Antigonish – or "Antigonowhere," as we outsiders liked to call it.

Last week I'd done a phone interview for a job in St. Paul, Minnesota. I was crossing my fingers that any minute now I would get an email or call from the department head.

Not that St. Paul would be so great. But at least, it was a city. There were bound to be non-white people there – what a concept! My students' last names wouldn't all be Macdonald, MacIsaac and Gillis. The place would have a Starbucks, a Gap, Thai restaurants and a movie theatre that played more than one film.

The St. Paul gig was just a two-year contract, hardly a plum career move. The days of peddling my trade, my suitcase overflowing with dog-eared syllabi, were hardly over. I'd be seventy before I landed a decent job. By then, I would be well published, albeit wrinkled and deranged, from decades of a bottle of wine a night and half-hearted flings with whoever was available.

Daddy coughed. "Well, it would be good to see you." He coughed again, like a hairball was caught in his throat.

"Yes?" I said. "Is there something else you want to say?"

"Things are changing here. You should see for yourself."

I waited for him to elaborate.

That was it? He expected me to put my summer research agenda on hold and fly to Toronto – at my own expense – simply because *things were changing?* Ever since he'd retired, he'd had way too much time on his hands. He'd taken up cooking, photography and other hobbies, but he was still bored. After decades of being a corporate high-flyer, calling me and my mother from airports in Santiago and Joburg, now, at sixty-three, he was turning into a touchy-feely homebody, yearning to recreate some long-lost sense of "home."

Freud had terms for this. Phantasm. Melancholia.

"Look, Daddy. I have to go. I've got a stack of papers I've got to mark by morning."

"It's your grandmother."

"What about her?"

"Leslie, why don't I call you tomorrow evening? You're sounding too wound up. Shaky or something. Is everything okay?"

"I'm *fine*. I'm just tired."

"Come home and relax. Think about it. We'll talk tomorrow."

A few minutes later, as I was in the midst of reading a terrible essay on Edith Wharton, a flash of curiosity cut through my dark office. I found myself distracted by curiosity about what he'd wanted to tell me about Granny.

I woke up at my desk, slouched forward, my face plastered to a sandwich wrapper. 11:55 My neck hurt and I had a splitting headache. The nightlights from the football field streamed in, casting an eerie glow over my books.

So much for marking papers.

I fumbled around for the light switch in the hall, and the pea-green walls lit up, sterile as a deserted hospital.

As I was waiting for the elevator, a bearded man appeared out of nowhere. My stomach did a back flip.

"Howdy," he said.

Just the caretaker. Standing a little too close, looking at me all too familiarly.

I rushed outside and stood on the cement piazza surrounding the front of the Arts Building. Beyond the empty parking lot loomed the low, undulating hills, which, for some strange reason, were called "the highlands." Although they didn't appear very high, they hemmed me in, filling my soul with desolation.

Maybe I would never get out. Incapable of publishing enough, I would perish.

These hills might as well be the Andes.

I crossed the little bridge suspended over an even tinier creek that marked the campus boundary, and continued on to Main Street. It looked exactly as you would picture a four-block stretch of downtown in any small town. Until moving here, I'd been familiar with such places only through movies like *New Waterford Girl* and *The Last Picture Show*.

A cool breeze washed over my skin, reminding me of a line from *Walden*: "This is a delicious evening, when the whole body is one sense, and imbibes delight through every pore. I go and come with a strange liberty in Nature, a part of herself."

I remembered how when I'd first been offered this job, I'd tried to make the best of it by imagining what awaited was a foray into pure nature. After all, if Thoreau could live for two years in a self-built cabin on Walden Pond, thriving in the heart of nature, gaining material for his famous memoir, what did I have to fear? Like Thoreau, I liked my solitude, so loneliness wouldn't be an issue. I related to his view that being surrounded by people and idle chatter often makes the individual feel lonelier than ever. I'd pictured myself going for long walks in the woods, communing with birds, brushing up against ferns, my ears attuned to every rustle and sigh. Nature would be my perfect companion.

Now I knew that was fiction and this was reality.

Reality was having to call in sick and take the bus all the way to Halifax to visit my therapist, Harriet, to deal with these "emergency" days that incapacitated me every so often. Days when I just couldn't bear to get up in front of the swarm of rosy, all too wholesome faces.

"I just don't know," I'd say to Harriet, as I curled up in the corner of her overstuffed sofa and cradled a hot mug, relishing the burning sensation. "I get up behind the lecture podium and take a deep breath, but the next minute I'm drowning in sweat."

She was a pudgy, blond woman, with sad lines fanning out around her eyes. She looked at me like she really did feel my suffering, but so far I'd been less than dazzled by her insights.

"If you hate your job so much, why don't you consider a career change?"

"And do what? I'm not qualified to do anything else. I'd be lucky if Starbucks would hire me."

Harriet was full of encouragement to "think positive." But the fact of the matter was that I was twenty-nine. The time for being unemployed, sponging off my parents, was long past. My dad would find me pathetic.

"Why would you assume you'll be unemployed for long? Lots of people go through career transitions."

She didn't know my father. She didn't know how practical and goal-oriented he was, along with everyone else in my family.

When I was five, my parents asked me what I wanted to be when I grew up. I promptly replied, "A writer."

My parents exchanged alarmed glances.

"How will you support yourself?" Daddy asked. "You *do* realize that writers barely make any money."

"You like pretty clothes and nice food," Mommy said, leaning so close I could smell her perfume.

All I knew was what my two-dollar-a-week allowance would get me at the corner store.

"Maybe I'll become a librarian, so I can be surrounded by books all day, and write my own books at night."

Mommy slowly nodded, but Daddy looked grumpy. "Why don't you become a lawyer and write books at night?"

No doubt, he was proud of the fact that I'd gone to McGill and Brown largely on scholarships, completing my B.A., M.A. and Ph.D. in record time – while costing him surprisingly little. But he was befuddled by my chosen discipline. To him, literature was an otherworldly, intangible realm about which normal people knew nothing. (He'd never read a book in his life, except for the Sparks Notes for *Macbeth* I found in the garage. Apparently, that was how he'd managed to pass his "English for Engineering Students" class in university).

"What are you going to do with all this education?" he asked. "Apply to law school?"

My saving grace was that I'd proven him wrong. My pile of degrees weren't useless; I was using them to become an English professor.

A glow came over my father's face when I first told him my plan. There was a certain prestige to being a professor – a "Dr. Somebody" – even in a field as esoteric as literature.

The next morning, I still hadn't heard back from the university in St. Paul. My palms were perspiring so much it was hard to type emails.

I looked out the window. Beyond the football field, a ribbon of highway curved past the cemetery, the harbour glimmering off to the left. It had once seemed so picturesque, yet it now appeared tainted with false illusions.

There must have been a moment when I realized I was in over my head, that my smile was about to crack. "Oh, no – I don't miss Toronto at all," I kept saying. Meanwhile, I couldn't stop scratching the welts from the swarm of killer mosquitoes that attacked me as I walked the two kilometres to campus every morning.

Ah yes, I could remember the moment. The moment when I realized that I was drowning in this cesspool of small-town bigotry.

It happened during office hours in the fall. A student leaned across my desk and peered in at me. The skin wrinkled up between his eyes as if he needed glasses.

Possibly, he did need glasses. He was a scruffy-haired scholarship student whose skin was covered in freckles, right down to his sharp elbows. Like many of the guys at St. FX, he reminded me of Huck Finn.

"Can I ask you something?" he said.

"Of course." I leaned forward, smiling. I was like Thoreau meeting his neighbours at Walden for the first time, fascinated by their coarse features and what thoughts glimmered behind the sleepy eyes. Often, I found myself watching these kids from the corner of my eye, as they hung out outside the library, sharing cigarettes, and something about the relaxed slouch of their shoulders and the way they laughed so loudly, right from the belly, made me think, as Thoreau had thought about his natives, that these kids didn't have an intellectual bone in their bodies.

And like Thoreau, I envied them. They had a freedom that we thought-tormented types could only dream about. I longed to be able to see the world with such purity.

Or so I thought, until the kid opened his mouth.

"What *are* you?" he said.

"What do you mean, *what am I*?"

He crossed his arms and looked down at his knees, as though he hadn't meant to say anything. The question had just popped out of his mouth. A moment earlier, I had been explaining the difference between British and American modernism.

"Are you Chinese, Japanese, Korean?"

My cheeks got hot and my wall of books shimmered – novels by James, Wharton and Conrad; volumes of poetry by Eliot, Pound and Moore; and theory books by Butler, Lacan and Derrida, to name a few. Suddenly they seemed nothing more than a rainbow of spines, empty of content. My art posters collected during the two years I'd spent in Berlin made me yearn for the city – any city.

So this was what it came down to. After all my years of study, after the endless hours poring over dusty pages in rare-book libraries, these kids weren't at all interested in what I had to say about literature. What they really wanted to know was where my ancestors had come from.

"Actually, I'm fourth-generation Japanese-Canadian," I said coolly. "My great-grandparents immigrated to Canada over a hundred years ago, and I don't speak Japanese at all."

"Do you miss it?"

"No – I've never been there. I mean I've never lived there. I visited Japan years ago, but I was just a tourist."

Confusion flickered on his face, followed by disappointment. Where he'd been expecting a story of being born to a concubine mother or nearly dying in a refugee camp, I was coming up short. But what could I say? I doubted he would be impressed if I told him that I barely survived two weeks in Saturday school before my mom pulled me out, because she didn't like the other Japanese-Canadian mothers, and enrolled me in Brownies.

He continued looking perplexed, and meanwhile I was thinking: Edith Wharton wasn't expected to yearn for the homeland of her Dutch ancestors, no one expects Henry James to pay tribute to his Irish heritage, and kid, *why am I trying to explain my identity to you anyway?*

I couldn't help it that my ancestral past was a big smudge. After so many generations in Canada, people in my family didn't tend to talk about it. And yet, I knew in my gut it was more than that. It couldn't have been fun growing up Japanese-Canadian in the years after World War II. Very rarely did my parents talk about their childhoods – as if it would be inauspicious to rehash the past – but I gathered that to survive, they'd learned to assimilate flawlessly so no one could ever again accuse them of not being Canadian. Apparently, when they were kids, a teacher had told my mom's older sister that Japanese was a "bad language," and after that my grandparents decided not to teach their younger children the language at all.

I knew that compared to the outright racism and schoolyard bullying my parents had endured, I had a lot to be grateful for, and perhaps it was only natural they'd shut out the past. Still, there was something about the silence they kept around our cultural background that had always bothered me.

But how could I begin to explain any of this to this kid in my office? And why would I want to? He flushed bright red and began sweating. Then I began sweating. He stumbled from my office and shortly after withdrew from my course.

Although I never saw him again, his look of curiosity and disdain stayed with me. Now I could see it glimmering on other students' faces, as I stood at the front of the auditorium lecturing on gender relations in Shakespeare and the figure of the madwoman in the Victorian novel. I looked out at the sea of dirty blond heads, and all I could see were freak show stares. They found it weird to see this Asian chick holding court on the geniuses of the Western tradition. It was as unnatural as seeing a white guy perform hip-hop.

10:31. I checked my email again. Still nothing. Ugh. I tore at a loose cuticle.

Outside the Arts Building, Peter Chisholm, a senior colleague, was trudging up the steps. His arms were laden with exam booklets. He smiled and I was struck by the way his thin lips curled inward, like the mouth of an old person without dentures.

"So how are your exams going?" he asked. "I just nailed my class on the Chaucer question." He made a hissing sound as if a bomb were hitting the ground. "Hmm. . . . I wonder whose grade just plummeted."

It occurred to me, not for the first time, that you really have to have a sadistic streak to enjoy being a professor.

"Students these days just spend all their time on Facebook and googling God knows what." Peter shook his head, smiling sadly.

We chatted a bit longer about the decline of education in our age – me nodding sympathetically, while zoning out – and at last I thought I'd endured enough to run off without making it too obvious. But he just wouldn't stop yapping.

"So you must be on cloud nine that your contract's been extended another year." In this job climate, Peter said, Harvard and Yale grads were clamouring for a kick at the can, even for adjunct positions at small colleges.

A searing pain cut across my sinuses, like I'd snorted chlorine swimming. The infuriating thing was that he wasn't exaggerating. It was depressing to read *The Chronicle of Higher Education*; the only thing it seemed to chronicle these days was how the situation worsened each day. Pay cuts. Faculty sit-ins. The marked drop in tenure-track job openings for professors – particularly those in English and foreign languages. After all, why hire profs on a full-year salary when you could rely on the ever-widening pool of adjuncts to work their asses off for nine-month contracts?

I flashed Peter a small, humble smile, and stared at the asphalt. "Oh yes, I'm glad that the department decided to keep me around for another year. It's a great university."

"Who knows?" Peter's eyes sparkled. "Maybe next year we'll get the funds to hire for your job as a tenure-track position. Of course I'm not guaranteeing that you'd be the successful candidate."

I smiled again. By now my cheeks were about to split.

Wobbling through the gravel in my stiletto sandals, I tried to hold back the tears. It would be embarrassing if students saw me in the midst of a meltdown, and I'd forgotten my sunglasses in my office.

12:06. Should I check my email again?

My heart stopped. Here it was:

> Dear Professor Shimotakahara,
>
> It was a pleasure interviewing you for the position of
> Visiting Assistant Professor of Modern American Literature
> last week. The department has concluded its deliberations,
> and decided to give the position to another candidate. We
> wish you all the best in your academic endeavours.
>
> Best regards,
> Mary Jo Steinbeck

✻ ✻ ✻

How long had I been staring at the screen, rereading the message? But there was nothing to interpret. The words were perfectly transparent.

Sunlight streamed in, pooling on my desk. Nevertheless, I felt incredibly cold, like I was at the bottom of a pit looking up at the last patch of sky. Waiting to be buried.

Until this point, I'd at least had a plan, a goal to keep me going.

Mrs. Wallace, the English department secretary, knocked on my door. "Your course evaluations," she said with a sunny smile.

"Great. Thanks." I backed away from my desk, where she'd placed the large manila envelope.

I knew it was a bad idea to read my evaluations at now of all times, but staring at the sealed envelope was too tempting. What did I know? We weren't always the best judges of ourselves. Maybe my terror was unfounded; maybe the students actually loved me. Or at least, one or two students.

Fingers trembling, I opened the envelope and stared at the rows of numbers on the first page – a summary of the Scantron scores that measured students' responses to questions about the general usefulness of the course material and the professor's ability to make the material interesting. 3.1, 2.9, 3.3. . . . God. Were these numbers on a scale of 5 or 10? I didn't even want to know. The numbers swam before my eyes, dizzying and shocking as some multiple choice test that I'd completely forgotten to prepare for. I couldn't continue reading. The humiliation was too vivid, too stomach-clenching.

Flipping through the questionnaires, where students had the chance to leave comments, I paused at a distinctive, slanted handwriting: "Dr. Shimo acts like she doesn't care about the students at all. Long silences loom over the class, in between her monologues which no one even understands. I'm beginning to doubt why I decided to take English."

The words hit me like a slap, but my outrage soon turned melancholy. I stuffed all the papers back in the envelope, which I shoved to the back of my desk, my pulse mounting with every second. But it was too late to hold back the tears. Here was the proof of my failure as a professor. Thanks to me, some poor kid was losing her love of literature. The extent to which I was unprepared for the depressing realities of this profession echoed down to my gut. When were things going to get better?

I rushed out the front doors, speeding past the familiar faces of students and colleagues, ignoring their puzzled smiles. I power-walked up and down Main Street. It was a stretch I'd come to know all too well. A bakery on the corner, a smattering of coffee shops, a diner, the one "good" restaurant where everyone went for special occasions, a video store, a Canadian Legion hall (I had no idea what this dreary grey building was, but I suspected it had something to do with the armed forces) and across the street, a brand-new Shoppers Drug Mart whose hulking red exterior was nothing short of blinding.

Where was the beauty of nature in all this? Or Nature, as Thoreau liked to call it, capitalizing its name like some magnificent deity. What a farce. Where was the lyrical experience of coming in touch with the earth that Thoreau had used to entice me here? *He* was to blame. During his self-imposed exile, he'd found a tranquility in solitude that, frankly, was beyond my grasp. He must have been deranged to glorify this social isolation. I recalled a section of *Walden* in which he wrote something about the pond "throwing off its nightly clothing of mist" – as if the friggin' pond was a beautiful woman slipping out of her negligee – and the whole thing suddenly struck me as so ridiculous I couldn't suppress a hysterical giggle. He turned Nature into the stuff of a trashy romance novel.

It was writing like that that had seduced me into thinking that some beautiful, higher level of consciousness awaited, if only I opened up my soul. The mysterious forces of the universe would flow in, imbuing my soul with a pseudo-religious, pseudo-orgasmic inspiration.

Yet in reality I was alone in the middle of nowhere. I had transcended nothing.

As I thought back to *Walden*, particularly the chapter called "Reading," I began wondering whether there wasn't something a little forced about Thoreau's insistence on being perfectly happy out in a cultural wasteland. Considering that Walden Pond is nowhere close to a library, as Thoreau grudgingly acknowledges, and his daily routine of digging in the garden leaves little time for reading anyway, doesn't his claim to being content ring hollow? The "slight insanity" he feels overtaking his mood, at one point, seemed like a grand understatement.

And what are the chances that his fellow men – country bumpkins – are going to learn Latin and Greek any time soon? In Thoreau's mind, true reading means one thing: reading the classics in their original language. He attacks how most men learn to read simply to take care of their banking, and nothing is more offensive than a little light reading for entertainment.

I couldn't imagine how he would have scoffed at my father's demand for a reading list. Reading as a retirement hobby would strike Thoreau as highly offensive.

But in the end, his stubborn elitism only serves to isolate him and push him to the edges of society. That was the sad truth about why he'd come to Walden.

Had the same thing happened to me? The thought was chilling.

Thoreau's renunciation of love – after his proposal to Ellen Sewall was rejected – and his claim to have no interest in pursuing law, the church, business or medicine, or any other profession open to a graduate of Harvard, took on a darker hue, as I thought about his fate compared to my own.

Incapable of dealing with the realities of modern life, had he felt just as isolated as me? How had he coped with the cold, lonely nights?

Where Thoreau had led a monastic existence, I had been all too willing to settle.

Pausing in front of the Town Hall, I stared up at a window on the second floor. Let's just say that I had a friend in Town Hall. An ex-boyfriend, to be exact.

Until a month ago, I had been dating Bobby Hawthorne, one of the mayor's coterie of advisors.

I'd met him at a faculty social in the fall, and at first I'd thought he looked like a geology professor. Auburn hair, a boyish smile, a muscular body, somewhere in his late thirties. He'd grown up in Fredericton, the centre of the universe by Maritime standards, and had travelled quite a bit in Europe. My heart leaped. I'd finally met someone whom I could actually envision dating here.

The first couple months of our relationship were sweet. There were times when I'd be staying at his place, out by the harbour, and the sheer beauty of the landscape filled me with a warmth that mingled with my ever-increasing affection for Bobby. He lived in a cottage-like house that he'd built with his own hands while living in a tent – how Thoreauvian was that? The house was even heated by a wood stove, and the view of the harbour sparkling through the kitchen window, the field shimmering with flecks of gold and purple, was worthy of *Walden*. Out back was a vegetable garden where Bobby planted potatoes, tomatoes and yes, beans, reminding me of the famous chapter called "The Bean-Field," where Thoreau chronicles his loving labours to yield nine bushels and twelve quarts.

Despite driving an SUV and a vintage convertible in the warmer months, Bobby considered himself a true woodsman. Once, I teasingly called him Thoreau, but he just looked at me blankly.

There were lazy Sunday afternoons, when we'd be trekking by the shore, and I'd be wearing a borrowed windbreaker and rubber boots (both a size too large, left behind by his ex-girlfriend), and looking at the postcard-pretty vista, my soul was filled with a great expansiveness, my ears attuned to the pattering drops of water, my eyes drinking in everything green, every pine needle expanding and swelling with a strangely orgasmic vitality. I'd look up at Bobby, my sexy woodsman, Thoreau-like, but minus Thoreau's bedraggled beard, and I'd thought to myself, *Life out here might really be okay*.

What did it matter that Bobby was no great intellect? He had little interest in talking about anything beyond cars, fishing and how much he loved the town, which meant we endured a lot of awkward silences during dinner. But I could shut out whatever blockheaded thing he was saying and pretend I was walking out here alone, immersed in perfect solitude. The sky swept down and kissed my face.

At that moment, it seemed that Nature was my ideal lover.

Poor, deluded girl.

Things began to sour between all three of us – me, Bobby and Nature – during the spring thaw. Bobby didn't understand why I was still hustling to get a job elsewhere.

The town had great growth potential, in his eyes. He was full of delusions about its future. The glory of the Internet, he claimed, was that it freed you from living in Toronto or Vancouver. Instead, you could live next to the river where you fished every day and work from your home computer.

One evening, I had too much wine and my true thoughts slipped out. "I hate to tell you this, but the locals aren't exactly welcoming to outsiders. Do you know how many people have told me I'm fresh off the boat?"

These days, I hardly batted an eye when I'd go to the shoe repair shop and be greeted with a booming "Konnichiwa," before being charged twenty-seven bucks for what should cost eleven dollars. I took for granted that whenever I'd run into a certain dean he would mistake me for a Chinese exchange student. The first time I met him, he put his hand on my shoulder and looked at me like I was a lost puppy, while asking if I needed help finding the ESL Centre.

"Well, that's natural." Bobby twirled his pasta. "You are exotic."

"What are you talking about?"

"You're different. You don't ski, you don't even know how to drive."

This had been a sore point between us. He thought I was insane for taking taxis to the supermarket. Meanwhile, I kept haranguing him to do something about the lack of public transit.

"And look at you," he continued. "You're obviously not Canadian. If you're not comfortable with that fact, maybe you should go home."

The cream sauce had congealed on my plate; it tasted bland as paste. *Home.* How I craved curry, kimchi, and wasabi – all the flavours of Queen Street. Anything to revive my anaesthetized taste buds.

Something crossed over in me, and I knew I had to get out. Looking down the road, imagining the next ten years of my life, I couldn't envision snowshoeing to work, eating slop and spitting out a brood of kids with this bigot. I despised him for not being the sophisticated, cosmopolitan guy I'd worked him up to be in my imagination. Not surprisingly, we broke up soon after, and my life since then had been pretty lonely.

I looked up at the planter of red geraniums outside Bobby's office window. They looked so cheerful and self-satisfied, flickering in the sun – I wanted to break their heads off and fling them in the gutter.

After giving my exam, I started walking back to my apartment. It was pitch dark, and the drunken hyena laughter of students rattled my already fraying nerves. When my phone buzzed, I tripped on the pavement.

Daddy. I had completely forgotten he would be calling.

"I didn't get the job in St. Paul." My eyes welled. My life was pathetic.

"Oh, well," he said. "I'm sure you'll figure it out. You're young. Your career will work out in the end."

That was the extent of his response to my crisis?

"Listen, I have to tell you something. It's your grandmother. She's been hospitalized."

"What's wrong?"

"Poison's in her blood. Her leg's going to have to be amputated, and who knows what else."

An ingrown toenail was to blame, he said. Due to a vascular problem, the blood in Granny's legs hadn't been circulating, so when her toe got infected, the wound couldn't heal and the whole thing turned gangrenous, spreading poison up her leg.

It was a shock to hear that Granny was declining so rapidly. All I'd known was that Daddy was concerned about her Parkinson's and memory loss. When I'd last seen him, he'd said there were certain things that he wanted to get on the record with her. Things about his childhood that she never talked about.

"Have you had a chance to talk with her about everything?"

"Not really." His voice went sullen as a child's. "It isn't easy to crack that woman's shell."

It was true that my grandmother was a strange woman. I often had the sense that I wasn't talking to a real person; her evasive glances and coy smiles seemed programmed, almost robotic. I had no idea what had made her this way, and after a while, I just chalked it up to the habit of a traditional Japanese woman. The Japanese doll that sat on her credenza had become intimately associated with her in my mind; it was as though, in some weird way, the doll *was* Granny. As a kid, I'd wanted nothing more than to play with that doll – run my fingers over her eggshell face, loosen the white sash on her red kimono to see how the draped layers would unfold. But of course I wasn't allowed to touch it. The doll was rare and valuable, Granny told me.

I knew that she was leaving me the doll in her will, even though I hadn't said I wanted it. The branch slung over the doll's shoulder frightened me. From the end of the branch dangled three masks: a beautiful woman, a demon, and a chubby-cheeked man who looked imposing enough to be an emperor.

"Do you want to come home to visit her?" Daddy asked. "It'll probably be your last opportunity."

"I could," I said slowly, "if you really want me to."

"It would be good for you to see her."

"Well, the semester's over. I guess I could fly back to Toronto."

No sooner had I said it than a ripple of anxiety crept across my chest. What was I thinking? Daddy's domineering attitude. Mommy's worried stares. At my age, it didn't seem natural to be going home for the summer.

Besides, I didn't want to see Granny's body chopped to pieces.

chapter two

And besides, what was there to go home to? Nothing but the silence of her cheerless room – that silence of the night which may be more racking to tired nerves than the most discordant noises: that, and the bottle of chloral on her bed.

-Edith Wharton, *The House of Mirth*

"Wow, nice job." I surveyed the white cupboards and marble floor that had replaced the wood and tile.

Daddy wheeled my suitcase in, and looked appraisingly around the kitchen. "Yeah, it turned out okay. At first, the contractor put in the wrong light fixtures, but I straightened him out."

"Did you get a discount?"

"What do you think?" His bushy eyebrows sprung up.

Before retiring, my father had been in charge of quality assurance for an international engineering firm. He still thought like he was on the job, rooting out places for cost cutting in home renovations, making Gantt charts to manage the schedule for recycling. Now that Granny was dying, he was probably getting quotes from funeral homes according to a price matrix of his own design.

Mommy looked me over, smiling.

Hugging her, I had a childish impulse to bury my face in her hair.

"Don't worry – I'm not going to wear out my welcome."

"Stay as long as you want," she said.

Daddy shot her a glance and I felt something tremble between them. Evidently, they'd been discussing my career blues.

Upstairs in my old bedroom, I examined the vine-and-violet pattern on the wallpaper that, at age eleven, had appeared the height of sophistication. Aside from the books and a small pile of CDs – Pearl Jam, U2, Portishead – the room was practically empty.

As I opened the closet, hangers rustled and old clothing greeted me like a retrospective. A puce taffeta dress that Mommy had sewn for me to wear to my junior-high graduation. A Strawberry Shortcake costume from the Halloween I was seven. Shoeboxes crammed with letters I neither wanted to throw away nor revisit.

This was the room of an aimless girl. Not the home of a worldly, well-educated woman.

And I hated how this house was full of mirrors. Sliding mirrors covered the closets in every bedroom. Unable to turn away, I stared at myself for a long time, like I'd never left this house at all. My hair looked dry as hay and my skin was ruddier than usual, and adjusting the low-rise waist of my jeans, my eyes paused at my bony hipbones, one jutting up higher than the other. I bent my knee and thrust my weight to the other side and put a hand on my hip, trying to disguise my imbalance. But it was pointless. A wave of hot frustration washed over my cheeks.

Leslie, why can't you stand up straight? The voice of my ballet teacher, who'd first noticed the problem, echoed in my head. She was the one who'd called my mother and set off the alarm bells. I breathed deeply and tried to push that whole miserable period from my mind, but the dull ache across my back had already set in.

Later, while Daddy was in the kitchen experimenting with his new wok, Mommy and I sat on the couch.

"He's been worse than ever since Granny was hospitalized," she said.

I smiled conspiratorially. Not that my mother needs encouragement to talk.

"Oh, he's been driving me bonkers! Yesterday, we were at the supermarket and he butted ahead of some nice old lady. 'I was here first,' he said. 'Excuse me, sir,' she said, 'but you were waiting for your wife, reading magazines.' 'I was not,' he shouted, and everyone looked over. I felt like dying of embarrassment."

"But that's nothing," I said. "That's Daddy on his good behaviour."

There were incidents far worse I remembered from childhood, when Daddy would bawl out waiters and demand discounts, and he'd been feuding with the neighbour for my entire life over who owned a pebbly strip between the two houses. My mom had to know she'd married a feisty guy, who would do and say whatever he wanted.

"Maybe he's on the spectrum," she used to say, meaning maybe he's on the Autism Disorder Spectrum (she'd read a study that showed many engineers were on the spectrum). He was obsessively fixed on his routines and favourite objects to the point he'd endangered his life. I remembered one of their biggest fights stemmed from his refusal to get a new car. He'd gotten attached to his old green Volvo and insisted on driving it into the ground. When he was driving home from a meeting one night, the car went up in flames on the side of the 401, just seconds after my dad grabbed his briefcase and jumped out.

While my mom was furious, Daddy appeared energized by the experience. She threw a fit, shouting that he had more than just himself to think about, but he retreated into a shell of silence, a mischievous smile playing on his lips.

Around that time, he took up building remote-control model airplanes, which became his passion in life. Ever since boyhood, he'd wanted to do this. Our basement quickly became crammed with his workbench and a dozen model planes – some of which were quarter-scale, making it hard to get to the TV. Every weekend and on weekday evenings when he didn't have to work late, he would drive to a landfill field out by Lake Ontario and fly his planes for hours. Once I went with him, but I was so bored, just staring at the sky. Yet I've never seen him so calm and content. He said flying his planes served a therapeutic purpose.

Mommy recommended that he try real therapy.

One night, he didn't come home for dinner. The sky was dark and it started to rain. Mommy paced around the kitchen and put away the food. Then she began calling his colleagues, but all anyone knew was that he'd left work early. I tried to stay calm and do my homework, but I couldn't concentrate. Had he been mugged or abducted on that dark field? Had he been struck down by lightning? Finally, Mommy put on her raincoat and said that she was driving there to start the search.

At that moment, Daddy came in. His hair was plastered to his forehead and his clothes were stuck to him, waterlogged and grey.

"My plane crashed in the lake." It was his favourite plane and he wanted to repair it. So he'd waded out into Lake Ontario, swimming through the polluted water trying to grasp on to the broken parts, until his feet could barely touch the bottom, but the smashed pieces kept floating further out. After a while, a cramp in his stomach made it hard for him to go on.

So he'd come home, depressed about losing his best plane.

Retirement must have made her soft in the head, if she thought that Daddy going ballistic on a nice old lady was anything out of the ordinary. Still, she insisted he was more erratic than ever since Granny's decline.

"But they weren't even close."

"It doesn't matter. You never can tell how a parent's decline will affect a person."

After a long pause, she asked, "But how are you?"

I was struck at that moment by how much Mommy had aged. She still wore the same shade of burgundy lipstick and her hair was freshly dyed, but the cut of her bob no longer appeared as impeccable. I could see the worry shining through her laugh lines, the faint bags under her eyes.

It was my fault. It caused her insomnia when I would call late at night, drunk and sobbing and full of pitiful stories about life in the boonies. I was selfish and self-absorbed, but I couldn't help it, and she indulged my need for an audience.

Maybe I was my father's daughter after all.

Daddy called us to dinner. Ginger and garlic wafted from the beef stir-fry he'd made based on his favourite dish in Chinatown. It actually smelled good. And it tasted good, too. He was enjoying my surprised expression.

"So what books did you teach last semester?" he asked.

"In my Am Lit class, we began with Thoreau, moved on to Sarah Orne Jewett and then wrapped up with Willa Cather and Ernest Hemingway. The modernists."

"Hemingway. Now there's a man's writer."

"Oh, I didn't know you've read him."

"I haven't, but I've always meant to." Daddy put down his chopsticks, his eyes flashing. "Weren't you supposed to put together a reading list for me?"

I laughed. He could get testy over the weirdest things. "Well, in case you haven't noticed, I've been a bit preoccupied."

"Oh, come on," Daddy said. "How bad can it be? You lie around reading all day and writing in a notebook."

"Excuse me?" Sweat broke out on my forehead.

"So your mother tells me you're thinking of jumping ship."

My eyes were getting soggy. Home for a few hours, and I was already losing it.

"Maybe you should try doing something more hands-on," Mommy said. "You don't seem to be thriving in the airy-fairy realm of literature."

I took a deep breath and tried to calm down enough to speak. But every time I opened my mouth, waves of despair tightened my throat.

"What are you so terrified of?" he asked. There was something different about the way he looked at me now, a glint in his eyes. Like I was a neighbour who'd parked in his spot or gouged his lawn.

"Everything," I hissed. "It's like the one thing I've been working toward all my life has been taken away. And now I have no idea what to do with my life. I'm like Lily Bart!"

"Who the hell is Lily?" Daddy said.

"She's – the heroine of – *The House of Mirth*." I couldn't manage to go on. My identification with her poor soul was too vivid, too horrifying.

Lily Bart begins as a poor little rich girl, indulged by her parents to believe that because they're old money, they'll always be the crème de la crème. But one day the party's over. When her father loses everything in a bad deal, Lily is faced with either marrying a fat cat or doing the unthinkable – working.

She tries to go it on her own, but like me, she's searching for her dream career, and the gigs that come her way – secretarial work, hat-making – just don't cut it. How I could relate to her rising desperation as her life becomes increasingly unstable and she sinks into dependency on the drug chloral.

One night she takes too much and accidentally kills herself – or was it suicide? No one knows. The mysterious tragedy of Lily Bart.

As I gave my parents a thumbnail sketch of her life, I was aware that their alarmed stares had more to do with me.

"Why do you identify with this tragic character?" Mommy said.

"Lily never finds her place in society. Everyone rejects her, she isn't good at anything, she ends up impoverished and alone."

"Well, that isn't going to happen to you. All your father and I want is for you to be happy."

I couldn't remember the last time I'd felt happy, or even gotten a good night's sleep. The walls of my stomach were constantly shifting; it was like living on a houseboat.

"Well, it's your life," Daddy said dismissively. "Do whatever you want. But don't expect a free ride."

"Free ride? All I'm asking for is a little support while I figure this out."

Daddy's lips tightened. "Well, how long is it going to take?"

The room was gently spinning, like I'd come through a revolving door too quickly. It was exactly like I'd told Harriet. He didn't care about my happiness at all. All he wanted was for me to be out of his hair, so he could travel, take up new hobbies and spend the bulk of his time flying his beloved planes.

He certainly didn't have time to play career counsellor to his screwed-up daughter.

"You do realize," I said, my voice trembling, "that this is the first time I've ever needed your help. What's the good of family if they're only there for you when you're getting awards?"

Daddy flushed.

"Don't worry, Leslie," Mommy said, glaring at him. "Look at you! Can you imagine the hell we'd be going through if we'd had a son?"

Daddy had always been grateful I'd been a girl. His relationship with his own father had been horribly conflicted, leaving him with doubts about whether he wanted kids at all.

"Don't baby her," he snapped. "She's a grown woman."

A few days later, Daddy was stretched out on the sofa reading. We hadn't spoken since the fight. He looked up and smiled, as though everything were back to normal.

"What's that?" I asked.

"*The House of Mirth.*"

Despite everything, guilt pinched at my nerves. He'd taken matters into his own hands and started the reading list without me.

"Let me know how you're finding it."

"Don't hold your breath," he said. "I read very slowly."

"That's good. *The House of Mirth* is the kind of novel you should luxuriate in."

Wharton's one of those rare writers who, from the moment I first read her, sent tingles all over my scalp and shoulders, right to my nipples. It was the familiar but still startling feeling of having your hair washed by someone who knows exactly where to rub and dig in her fingernails. I could almost smell the aromatic shampoo wafting up from the salon sink. That's the toe-curling effect of reading Wharton.

Despite her florid vocabulary and sentences so complex they seem acrobatic, it was as though a kindred voice whispered from beneath the page, and I thought, She really gets me. If she were alive now, I was sure we'd be friends. We'd be swinging our legs on barstools, sipping martinis.

What other novelist has created a heroine who projects such an intense aura? More than simple beauty or good taste, Lily Bart has an indescribable quality that seems to emanate from her very flesh, like a soft light. It isn't sex per se; Lily, at age twenty-nine, is a virgin, despite the fact that she wears low-cut gowns and keeps company with the Donald Trumps of the world. Yet sex appeal has everything to do with her unattainable beauty.

Daddy looked like a student studying for an exam. His watch was propped on the coffee table so he could see exactly how long he'd been reading. Ever since he'd taken up this new hobby, he was very precise about reading every day for a full three hours.

"Why is Lily Bart such a basket case?" he said, as I walked by.

Day by day, as I sat at my childhood desk, I could feel myself slipping. I couldn't bring myself to return emails from old friends – smart, practical friends who'd seen the writing on the wall and bailed on English literature after one degree and gone on to law school and HR certificates. Their career prospects were soaring with job offers in New York and business trips to Frankfurt, while I languished in this dead-end profession.

Maybe that was why Wharton spoke to me. She knew how to make beauty of the mess that misguided, bleary-eyed girls make of their lives.

One afternoon as I was wandering through the neighbourhood – I had time on my hands for long nostalgic walks – I went into my favourite used bookstore. And there was a dog-eared copy of *The House of Mirth*.

Reading the opening paragraph was like rediscovering an old perfume. "Selden paused in surprise. In the afternoon rush of the Grand Central Station his eyes had been refreshed by the sight of Miss Lily Bart." From there, the intriguing images unfold, from Lily's "desultory air" to her "air of irresolution which might, as he surmised, be the mask of a very definite purpose" to Selden's fascination with "the modelling of her little ear, the crisp upward wave of her hair." Everything about this woman, from her unpredictable moods to the minute details of her appearance, catches Selden's fancy. Yet he's aware that he's "far out of her orbit." He's like the nice, nerdy guy in high school who befriends the cool, popular girl by flirting when she's had a bad day and offering to do her homework.

The thrall and mystery of female beauty. What woman doesn't secretly desire such power?

A guilty pleasure, no doubt. As modern women, we've supposedly transcended such nonsense – the vanity, the narcissism, the endless desire to be desired. Long evolved beyond all that, we're supposed to be rushing off to meetings dressed in tailored suits, staying up late to write the Long-Term Plan, kicking butt at the Curriculum Committee Meeting. Yet Wharton's brilliance is that she can awaken flutters in even the most liberated of readers by showing what it would feel like to possess, vicariously, Lily Bart's power and vulnerability, immersed in the milky, mesmerized gaze of some perfect admirer.

I remembered when I first started really enjoying sex (by this point, I was on my third boyfriend, Joshua Goldman). It had everything to do with seeing that look on Josh's face, as he shoved a firm pillow beneath my butt and his eyes swept over my flesh. I revelled in relinquishing control, and the suspense was irresistible. All the boring, familiar aspects of my body – my knobby knees, my sharp hipbones – took on a new interest as I saw how much they fascinated and delighted this freckle-faced boy.

For the first time, I felt sexy.

God, I really had to stop doing this. I had this embarrassing habit of thinking of characters in novels as real people.

In grad school, this is the first thing you're taught never to do. It's an absolute faux pas. To read assuming that literary characters are flesh-and-blood human beings, with feelings and desires like you and me, is considered without a doubt the lowest form of reading. Biographies and autobiographies might be fine for the book-of-the-month club, but they have no place in academia, especially at the upper echelons.

Or so my revered mentors at Brown had taught me.

During my Masters and Ph.D., I was given a repertoire of more sophisticated tools for understanding literature. I took seminars on post-structuralism, deconstruction, new historicism, queer theory, psychoanalysis, and Marxist cultural theory, to name just my first-year course load. We did Freudian readings of Woolf and Marxist readings of Freud and debated whether post-colonial literature let the subaltern speak. Sitting around the fireplace in Carr House, we drew diagrams of massive layer cakes where each layer was meant to represent another tier of ideology. Late at night, drunk on red wine, we got into huge fights about whether literature could only be grasped as a reflection of its historical period or whether literature illuminated grand philosophical concepts that transcended history altogether. This was how I'd been trained to think, ripping every text into strands of discourse.

But why did I always feel like *I* was unravelling around the edges?

To an up-and-coming literary scholar, literature certainly wasn't supposed to be about sympathizing with Thoreau because he couldn't get laid or fantasizing a rewarding career for Lily. Duh. Reading to make friends with characters in your head was more than a tad sophomoric. But the truth of the matter was that after all this study, I'd never been able to shake my natural tendency to read for precisely this reason. In my heart of hearts I'd never bought into the academic style of reading.

As a professor, I was a phony.

"You need to make a list of all the things you're looking for in a new career," Mommy said. We were having lunch at a café around the corner, nibbling on soggy focaccia.

"Remember that I wasn't always a speech-language pathologist," she continued. "I found it in the Yellow Pages."

It was a story I'd heard many times before. Years before I was born, my mom had had a short-lived career as a high-school French teacher. Barely fluent, she had gotten the job as a fluke and could never get past her feelings of incompetence. One day, she was looking through the phone book and came across, quite by accident, "Speech Therapy." The term caught hold in her mind and she cold-called someone to request an information interview.

She loved being a speech-language pathologist, chaired committees, designed school curricula and over the years rose to the top position – Chief of Speech-Language Pathology.

"Make a list," Mommy said, reaching for a pen.

"Lily reminds me of you," Josh once said to me. We were sitting at the Second Cup across the street from McGill. I was reading *The House of Mirth* for the first time; it was on the syllabus of my Women's Lit class.

"What do you mean?"

He continued flipping through the novel, reading random passages, an assured smile playing on his lips.

This was the nature of our relationship. He was five years older and always seemed authoritative, even when I knew he was talking out of his ass. Maybe this was because he'd given me a lot of firsts: my first orgasm, my first taste of *strega*, my first lesson on how to use chopsticks properly. I was dumbfounded when he told me that I shouldn't hold my chopsticks so close to the base or let them crisscross unless I wished to be seen as a peasant. As if he knew more about being Japanese than I did. He was full of these peculiar tidbits of knowledge he'd picked up from reading book reviews in *The Economist*.

"You and Lily are both hot chicks and you're both also kind of . . . rudderless."

"Rudderless?"

I licked the syrup off the top of my caramel machiatto and tried to act normal. Josh shrugged and started pontificating about a micro-finance lecture.

My cheeks grew hot and oily. The grilled mushroom sandwich I'd had for lunch was mixing with the caramel and coffee, a weird, sludgy science experiment in my stomach.

Rudderless?

It was true that I had no idea what I wanted to do. All I knew was what I didn't want to do. I couldn't bear to spend my life under the laundromat-bright lights of a lab (I had already transferred out of the B.Sc. program), and the thought of applying to law school was no less deadening. So I read. I was doing an entire degree that consisted of nothing other than reading useless works of literature.

My mind had always been drawn to frivolous activities, I was coming to realize, and although my mom assured me it was only a matter of time before I figured things out, I was terrified I'd never get beyond this morass of vague, unarticulated aspirations.

Did I resemble Lily? Did this mean that I would never be happy? That I had a self-destructive impulse at the core of my being?

"You should become an English prof," Josh said to me one morning, as we were sitting across from each other in McLennan Library. He looked so pleased with himself, his cheeks glowing, and I thought, *This must be how you look when you're having an epiphany.*

"What do I know about teaching?"

"Who said anything about teaching? If you're any good as a prof, you barely spend any time in the classroom. You're roaming around Europe doing your research and hibernating in libraries and sitting at sidewalk cafés sipping your espresso. It's a pretty phat life."

It was just another of his off-the-cuff ideas, but it caught hold in my mind.

Why don't you become an English prof?

Only a girl who was truly rudderless would be drawn to the idea.

In a flash, my fate was sealed. That bastard.

Granny lived two and a half hours away in Niagara Falls. Traffic was dreadful, and I fell asleep in a weird position. By the time we got there, I felt like a zombie. As we entered the sterile building, the feeling intensified. Something about pea-green walls.

At least Granny had her own room. Someone had arranged yellow chrysanthemums in a giant Coke cup.

Ted McCabe, Granny's second husband, got up from where he'd been sitting in the corner watching *Jeopardy*, and ambled over. Crumbs were caught in his roughly clipped beard.

Granny was asleep under a rainbow afghan, her body as small and frail as a child's. Her leg had not yet been amputated; we were giving the medication one last go. Her dyed black hair was flat and greasy, and her lips had fallen open, like a droopy tulip.

Everyone said she'd been beautiful when she was young. Even after the war, when the Japanese-Canadians were considered traitors, men still looked adoringly at Granny. Strangers on the street opened doors and helped her onto the streetcar, while my dad hid behind her skirt.

Suddenly Granny's eyes flew open, her lashes fluttering. "Where am I? Where is Blackie?"

"She's been like this all morning, calling out for her old dog," Ted said.

Two hours later, we were still waiting to talk to her doctor. The TV droned on, strident and predictable. I dozed off.

When I woke up, Daddy and I were alone with Granny. Through the fringe of my half-closed eyes, I could observe him tearing apart a Styrofoam cup.

"How have you been sleeping?" he said.

"Every night, out like a light."

His eyes lit up at her lucid reply. "That's not what the nurse told me. She says you've been waking up, screaming out. Like when I was a child. Do you remember that, Mom?"

"I've always slept well."

"That's not what I remember." Daddy wandered over to the dresser and began examining her bottles, messing them up, clinking glass.

"Oh, right," he continued. "We were one big happy family. A lovely family, the neighbours used to say. Kaz was out of work and losing his mind, but you covered up for him. You put on lipstick and curled your hair and deluded yourself that everything was okay."

"The neighbours are talking about us?" Alarm crossed her face.

"Oh, yeah," Daddy said. "The walls were thin – I'm sure they could hear everything. Don't you remember how Kaz used to storm around the house?"

"I don't remember anything like that."

"What are you doing, Daddy?" It was the first time I'd ever seen my father talk openly about the past.

He pulled from his pocket something that looked like a tiny cell phone and held it in front of her lips. "Mom, think hard. *Think* about what I'm asking you."

"What is that?" I asked.

"It's a digital recorder. I've been taping our conversations at the nursing home over the past year."

He'd been taping their conversations. He said it so casually, as though it were normal behaviour to be investigating his mother.

"What are you after, Daddy?"

"It's good to talk about the past."

"But what are you really after?"

He pressed the pause button, his cheeks flushed. "All my life, 'I don't remember, I don't remember.' How can she say that? *She was there.*"

"You want to understand Granny," I said.

He nodded. "I want to know the real Masako Shimotakahara."

There was something about his perplexed, petulant expression that reminded me of how Selden, Rosedale and all Lily's other admirers must have felt – fascinated and frustrated by the enigma of the real Lily Bart. It occurred to me it was oddly fitting for Daddy to be reading this novel, given his strange obsession with Granny.

What is this woman trying to hide? What does she truly want? Why won't she act rationally to save herself? The same questions that make *The House of Mirth* such a page-turner had been simmering at the back of my father's mind.

Daddy's chest puffed out as he got ready for another round of interrogations, and the whole thing was making me really nervous. What if he flew off the handle and the nurse called security?

"What did you dream about after Kaz was gone?" he asked. "Did you

35

imagine that he was still alive, chasing you around the house?"

"Kaz was never the same after his stroke."

"I'm sorry I never got to meet my grandfather," I said. "I'm sure he was nice before he got sick."

It used to seem strange that Daddy referred to his father by his first name. All my friends, when I was little, had grandpas – or at least stories about grandpas who'd died in wars and hunting accidents. All I had was this man called "Kaz," who'd popped off when Daddy was a young man. Whenever someone mentioned his name, Daddy's face would tighten like a fist.

"He wasn't nice," he said. "I'm glad you never had to meet him."

"It was the stroke," Granny said.

Usually, he and Granny never talked about anything more consequential than movies and TV shows. But now, there was something serious he wanted to say to her, and he was like an inarticulate child.

I felt protective of my father as though I were seeing him through the eyes of a social worker: a neglected child crying out for his mother's attention.

A week later, Daddy and I were sitting at the kitchen table over breakfast. I hesitated, swept some crumbs into my palm.

Finally, I asked him whether he liked the novel.

His lips twisted, somewhere between a smile and a snarl. "Wharton's sentences are way too long and twisty. And what do I care whether a pillow is satin or velvet?"

"Okay." It was good to get him expressing his views. It was a start. I was glad that he was reading as a distraction from his weird investigation of Granny. "What else are you noticing about the text?"

"I have no idea why that wimp, Selden, is so hung up on Lily Bart. He just follows her around like a little kid, full of big ideas that he alone gets the real Lily Bart. No man thinks like *that.*"

"Could you give me an example?"

He flipped through the novel, raising his eyebrows. "Oh, how about here? This is the part after they've had the big fight at the ball, and Selden's left town. But then they run into each other overseas in Monte Carlo. It's ridiculous how Selden describes being heartbroken. Seeing Lily, he talks about her skin as if it's cold porcelain – beautiful, but a turn-off. What man talks that way? I challenge you to find me one guy, who isn't a gay art critic."

"Okay, maybe you've got a point. Wharton was writing from a woman's perspective, imagining how Lily – or Wharton herself – wished to be seen by a male spectator."

I launched into a mini lecture about the dynamics of voyeurism, but all the while I was thinking: it really came down to Wharton's intimacy issues. She never experienced true desire and fulfillment. Her marriage at age twenty-three to Teddy Wharton, one of her set, was a sham from the outset. A womanizing alcoholic without an intellectual bone in his body, his indiscretions pushed Wharton over the edge. Following her breakdown, they divorced. While Wharton proved more resilient than her alter ego, Lily, the sadness and vulnerability she projects through her heroine had a source from within.

The coterie of friends and writers who surrounded Wharton in the latter half of her life provided some compensation. But one never gets the sense in reading her letters to Henry James that their intellectual banter, replete with flirtation and innuendo, could progress beyond a certain point (it later turned out that James was struggling with his own torments, living in the closet). With the exception of a short-lived affair with a married reporter – whom James also lusted after – Wharton appears to have lived a largely celibate life. The closest she ever came to love was probably her lifelong friendship with Walter Berry, a lawyer, like Selden. Wharton and Berry shared much in common through their passion for books, languages and architecture, and they'd had a dalliance during their youth. She'd once entertained hopes that Berry would propose, but he never acted upon the idea.

Yet in her tribute to Berry after his death, she wrote that he walked on water. *He found me when my mind and soul were hungry, and he fed them till our last hour together.* . . .

Thwarted, their love was complete. And so it is, in all her great novels. Ultimately, Wharton's addiction to tragedy and pathos trumps her desire for intimacy and a happy ending.

A complex, contradictory woman. She never quite figured out what she wanted in a lover.

Had I? Did I suffer from intimacy issues, too?

When I wanted to be alone with my own thoughts, a shroud came over my entire personality and the tiniest distractions – the TV, even the sound of someone breathing – could throw me into a rage. Immersed in Adorno and Faulkner, I didn't give a shit about my boyfriend. I was impossible, but I couldn't change. My life had a higher purpose, I told myself.

"You're leaving me to read books?" That was what Josh had said to me the last time I saw him, seven years ago. We were having dinner at his favourite restaurant, a tiny *izakaya* on the Lower East Side.

He'd invited me to New York for the weekend. We hadn't seen each other since we'd broken up two years earlier in Montreal, after he'd graduated. Since then, he'd been living in Japan, teaching English and dabbling in the first half of a Masters in Japanese history, but he was back in New York for good. NYU had accepted him for law school.

I sipped my sake and enjoyed the rush of warmth. "You were the one who convinced me to become a prof in the first place."

"Yeah," he said. "I just wish you were at grad school here. Rather than at that little unknown community college in Rhode Island."

"Hey, don't insult Brown. It's good enough for the Kennedys."

There was a new resoluteness to his jaw line, a new seriousness to the way he looked at me. "It would be fun if you were here. Like old times. Who knows what might happen?"

I smiled and chewed a morsel of rubbery octopus. Two years ago, I'd longed to hear those words. But now, they hardly caused a stir. In fact, it was annoying to see him looking at me that way.

I had Wharton, James and Eliot now. If the life of the mind required going it alone, I was certain that the rewards would be worth it.

Naïve, silly girl. Now I knew that the life of the mind wasn't worth shit.

Why was Josh on my mind all of a sudden? All the poignant moments of our relationship kept replaying in my head, like a montage at the end of a Woody Allen movie. Everything that had been lost. Everything that might have been.

During one of my long walks around Toronto, it occurred to me that this was the first time in quite a while that I was without a boyfriend. I'd become the kind of woman who always had someone, no matter how inadequate, no matter how mismatched.

But now I was all alone. I missed having a boyfriend, but I missed no one in particular. My libidinal energies were loose and aimless.

The basement apartment Josh had rented in New York had a tiny bathroom in the corner with just a curtain in the doorway. No door. I remembered noticing this when we went back to his place that night, drunk on sake.

We started kissing, and the thing I was most aware of was the distance between our bodies. Shadows played on his arms as light through the window pooled on the cement floor, a queer, underwater sensation.

We weren't going to make it; we could both feel it in our bones. There was a boredom – a hopelessness – to all our gestures, even as we tried to excite each other with the old tricks.

If he was right that I resembled Lily, he by implication must be Selden. As I thought about it, the parallels mounted, most vividly in their last scene together. By that point, Lily has fallen out of society – her reputation has been irreparably tainted by her scandalous association with rich, married men. Most painful is her falling out with Selden. In the final days of her life, as her health deteriorates, she finds that she still longs to see him, and one evening drops by his flat.

Yet nothing is resolved through their bittersweet rapprochement.

Later that evening, as Lily lies in bed, indulging in an extra-high dose of chloral, her final thoughts are of Selden, and she's plagued by the feeling that something is still to come. She's drifting in and out of consciousness and all she can think is that there's something she has forgotten to tell Selden – something she should say to make their love clear.

My thoughts were no less muddled, as I curled up later that night in Josh's bed, hugging the sheets around me, clinging to the wall. After we'd made love, he'd gone out like he'd been given an injection. Yet I had a queasy, unsatisfied feeling in my stomach, as though I'd gone to bed without eating.

I'd been expecting a sense of closure. By sleeping with him one last time, I was seeking confirmation that yes, we were never right for each other.

But instead I was left with insomnia and an upset stomach.

It didn't matter that I would leave him and bury myself in my studies, because he would still be with me through fantasized conversations.

I wanted it to be over, yet it wasn't. Maybe it would never be over, this feeling of wanting more. But more of what? All I knew was that he always left me with the excruciating sense of something left unsaid.

chapter three

In the dark of my room I imagined that I saw again the heavy grey face of the paralytic.

-James Joyce, *Dubliners*

I'd been lying on the sofa for hours. Why hadn't anyone invented meal capsules? I couldn't bear the pointlessness of getting up to fix a sandwich, only to sit there, eating it by myself.

Rain was pattering on the slanted glass of the solarium. As a kid, I used to love this room. "I live in a glass house," I'd brag to kids at school. But now, the glass, wet and blurry, assumed another quality.

My grandmother's funeral was bound to be any day.

My parents had gone to Niagara Falls, but I'd stayed home to get my shit together. My mom was on my case to make that list and check out career-counselling websites.

But all I did was take long walks.

Something about the street appeared different. Every little change to Glenforest Road had added up to a new look and feel, but I'd somehow missed the shift. What had become of those decrepit little houses with peeling paint and lawns no one mowed? I remembered the wildflowers rising to my waist. But Daddy had raged at property prices being dragged down and he was glad when the old ladies croaked.

Turning onto Yonge, I was struck by the disappearance of the fish and chips shop. It had been replaced by an Indian restaurant with a glowing *Toronto Life* review in the window. I hadn't gone for fish and chips in years, but I found it unsettling that the place had vanished. My eyes teared up, rain stinging my cheeks. As I walked south toward Lawrence, more of the familiar places were nowhere to be seen. What had happened to that convenience store where the guys at school used to buy porn? What had become of the sweet, chubby face of that Korean lady behind the counter?

As the days went on, I ventured further. I wandered past the old people's home, all the way to Coffee Time Donuts. It brought back fond memories of Friday nights in high school, when I'd sat around with friends chatting for hours. Being out late anywhere without one's parents was glorious back then. A double-double and a cigarette that someone had stolen from her sister's purse were all it took to make us happy. The evening was set. But now you couldn't even smoke in that sanitized air.

My oldest friend, Clara Kim, found out I was in town. I'd known her since kindergarten – a bold little girl with a secretive smile and a big laugh to compensate. Her parents had been chemists back in Korea, but they'd sacrificed everything so the kids could enjoy the good life. She'd sidled up to me in the schoolyard and let me know that just because I lived in a big house and she lived above a convenience store, I shouldn't think that I was any better than her.

I wouldn't have dared. I was an awkward, timid kid with my hair in a bowl cut. It was a miracle anyone was talking to me at all.

Our friendship had had its ups and downs over the years, and I wasn't at all sure I wanted to see her. But here we were, at a brand new pan-Asian restaurant on Bloor. The waitress seated us at a bright white booth, against which Clara's skin glowed bronze.

"Oh, Les, we have so much to catch up on." Naturopathy school had opened her eyes to the world – she warned me of the perils of processed foods. She'd even converted Jim to a "veg." I wondered how he managed to take his clients out to dinner.

Sun poured in the window, a stream of harsh brightness, and the afternoon went on longer than I would have liked.

On my way home, the old neighbourhood library beckoned to me, but inside the air smelled mildewy as a funeral home. I sunk into a lounge chair across from a homeless woman reading *Elle*. The big clock went tick-tick, like back in school when we'd be counting the seconds until class dismissed.

The homeless woman had on Tretorns so dingy, they were more grey than pink. The same shoes I'd worn back in grade four.

As soon as she got back, Mommy set up a slew of information interviews, based on the points I'd jotted down:

1) employment in Toronto

2) don't need to drive

3) does not involve physical labour

4) does not require bullshitting students about how reading great works of literature will make you a better person

It wasn't much, but she could work with anything. She arranged a bunch of lunch dates with friends who were speech-language pathologists and a policy analyst at the Ministry of Colleges, Universities and Training.

My mom's friends were perfectly nice, although perplexed.

"I thought you were off teaching in Nova Scotia," a woman named Janet said. "Your mom always brags about you being a professor. What made you change your mind?"

As I picked at my salad, I wanted to climb under the limp leaves. This interview was going nowhere. Maybe I'd apply for a job as a telemarketer, like some refugee.

A refugee from academia. That was me.

"What should I read next?" Daddy asked.

He looked pleased at my surprised expression.

"He so enjoyed *The House of Mirth*," Mommy said. "You've got to recommend something else."

Perhaps it was his way of extending an olive branch, or more likely, Mommy had given him a talking-to. I could hear her saying, "Don't you want to be close to Leslie? You've got to *reach out*." So now they were trying to snap me out of my funk with their over-animated looks.

Fine. I could rattle off titles by the dozen. Just as long as they didn't expect a lecture.

"Why don't you try Joyce's *Dubliners*?" I had a copy on my old bookshelf.

"Joyce?" Daddy looked worried. "Years ago, I flipped through *Ulysses* at a friend's apartment. Man, those sentences are long."

People tend to approach Joyce with about as much enthusiasm as a root canal.

"Don't worry – *Dubliners* is nothing like *Ulysses*. Consider it a kind of 'Joyce Lite.'"

I explained that both works share in common certain themes, such as Joyce's rant against Ireland being a cultural wasteland. But the styles of *Ulysses* and *Dubliners* are entirely different. *Dubliners* was written before literary style went all experimental in the 1920s and became impossible for normal people to understand.

Although everyone waxes lyrical about the brilliance and timelessness of *Ulysses*, deep down I'd always preferred its simpler little brother. Lacking the epic pretensions of *Ulysses*, *Dubliners* is just a collection of short stories about the lives and ways of people in Dublin.

"Trust me, you'll like it."

He didn't look convinced.

My choice wasn't entirely random – there was something about this book that reminded me of Daddy. The grittiness of Dublin. The isolation of all the characters. A cloud hangs over the city. Musty drawing rooms, dingy streets, boarding houses full of all kinds of unsavoury types.

I didn't know much about my father's childhood, but I knew he'd grown up in the ghetto. Before the war, the Shimotakaharas had been one of the old, well-respected Japanese-Canadian families in Vancouver, but not many wanted to stay in B.C. after the internment, according to my great-aunt Tetsuko, Kaz's little sister. Those who could went, wherever the train would take them – Montreal, Toronto, Hamilton, wherever. Anywhere that offered a fresh start.

So my father was born in Verdun, a slummy part of Montreal, and later the family moved to Toronto, the Bloor-Lansdowne area. The 1950s wasn't the greatest time to be Japanese-Canadian, and he seemed to have spent a lot of time alone.

The opening story, "The Sisters," portrays a boy investigating the death of his friend, the local priest. It's evident as he tours the neighbourhood that everyone thinks the boy is weird for being friends with Father Flynn – a bedridden bogeyman. In the end, Father Flynn's paralyzed body provides a kind of symbol for the whole community, making the boy feel more alienated than ever. Every night, he repeats the word *paralysis* with the solemnity of a religious ritual, rolling the word around in his mouth.

Paralysis, paralysis, paralysis. I could picture my dad as that boy.

My eyelids grew heavy.

June was the month I slept a lot.

One night after dinner, Aunt Wendy called. Her voice was so shrill I could hear her through the receiver, as Daddy tried to calm her down.

The medication hadn't been working – Granny's leg had to be amputated on the spot.

The next morning, we drove to Niagara Falls. The surgeon said he hadn't been able to spare her knee due to the extent of the infection. Besides, there didn't seem much point. At her age, she'd never walk again.

It was strange to think that only one high heel would poke out from under the afghan.

When we entered her room, the first thing I noticed was she wasn't wearing a trace of makeup. It was as though all her flesh had been suctioned out, leaving a sagging, bare canvas. And not a hint of perfume. All I could smell as I leaned over the bed to embrace her was the alcohol from the wipes. She smelled like a sickly baby.

A blanket covered her legs, tracing the outline of the stump. But if I hadn't known, I might have just thought that her leg was curled up. Looking at it made the tender parts of my body sore.

"Granny, does it hurt?"

"What?" Her lashes fluttered without a trace of recognition. "I don't remember."

Daddy whispered something in her ear.

"Who's there? Jack, it's you, Jack."

"Yes, mom."

"You need to collect the rent." Her eyelids twitched.

"What are you talking about?"

"The boarders."

"What boarders?" I said.

"The German man owes us money," Granny said.

Daddy rubbed the back of his neck. "She's talking about the house on St. Clarens, where we used to live."

"It was a boarding house?"

He nodded. "Kind of like Mrs. Mooney's."

"What are you talking about?"

"Joyce."

Oh, right. He was talking about "The Boarding House," one of the stories in *Dubliners*. Mrs. Mooney is the woman with a great florid face. To

46

compensate for her loutish drunk of a husband, she turns her house into a boarding house and it attracts a host of bachelors, thanks to her pretty daughter, Polly.

The story turns on Polly's seduction – which Mrs. Mooney practically orchestrates by parading her around the house. When she has proof that her daughter has been seduced, she takes a distinct pleasure in sitting the young man down. Mr. Doran's life passes before his eyes – his every instinct tells him once you're married it's all over – but the terror of answering to Mrs. Mooney overwhelms him. It doesn't take her long to browbeat him into marriage.

"Things like that happened in your house?"

"You don't know the half of it."

I wanted to press him, but Granny started trembling, calling out for more drugs.

Daddy had a new hobby. He'd become obsessed with websites on the Japanese-Canadian immigrant experience. Late at night, I found him sitting at his desk, the grainy, black-and-white faces of strangers glowing on the screen.

Farmers wearing rice-picker hats. Self-satisfied matrons standing outside some bakery. Little boys in white baseball uniforms running around a dusty square in an internment camp. The captions told a familiar story of struggle and dispossession, with the resilience of the community always prevailing.

"What do you find so fascinating about these pictures?" I asked.

"This is our past we're talking about."

I nodded, yet I had to admit these photos didn't do much for me. It wasn't like I felt any personal connection to these people. It creeped me out to see my father staring at the images for hours.

I felt in my gut that the mystery he was trying to unravel had its origins closer to home.

I went with Daddy to visit Granny again. It didn't take long for him to start his interrogation.

"Before you got ill, Mom, you started to tell me about how you met Kaz."

"I don't remember."

"Mom, *think* about it."

There was a long silence, while her eyelids fluttered. A butterfly on the verge of dying.

Daddy scowled.

Finally, Granny said, "I won a beauty contest for Japanese girls on the West Coast."

"How old were you?"

"Fifteen, maybe."

"You became friendly with the boys very early. So Kaz heard about your reputation? Is that why he drove all the way from Vancouver to Portland?"

She smiled faintly.

"Did Kaz meet you at the pageant?"

She shook her head. She said that one day when she was watering the flowers outside the house in Portland, Oregon, where she grew up, a young man pulled up in a black car. It was Kaz with a bunch of friends in the back. Since they'd heard the dancing was good in Portland, he said, they'd driven down for the weekend.

"They were looking to meet Japanese-American girls," Daddy said. "Did he ask you out?"

"Not really. He just sat in his car, smiling and watching me. And I recognized that car. I'd seen it outside my house before."

"You mean Kaz was *stalking* you."

"He liked pretty girls."

Daddy looked disgusted. "Kaz was already sick."

"What's sick about liking a pretty girl?"

It amazed me that her face could remain so composed while my father bristled and prodded her. But he couldn't get to her, he couldn't shatter her surface. What was going on in her mind? She was like a child who deals with being punished by retreating to a fairytale land in her head.

"Even then, he was a sicko," Daddy said.

She lay back and closed her eyes.

Granny had given Daddy a photo album for his sixtieth birthday. "This Is Your Life," read the title page in her shaky writing, garlands doodled around the edges. I remembered Daddy had rolled his eyes and put it on the top bookshelf in the living room.

These photos mesmerized me.

In the first picture, Granny is perched on the edge of the bed, clasping a newborn against her bosom. What woman wears lipstick after having just given birth? Her smile is as vivacious as Rita Hayworth's, framed by a cascade of dark curls.

Yet there's something frightened about her face. Fear flickers in her eyes like light across pools of water, her smile about to dissolve.

Another photo in the album is a picture of a house with a large front porch. My dad, as a young teenager, is sitting on the sagging steps, looking surly.

"Is this the house on St. Clarens?" I asked.

Daddy looked up from his book. "I'm reading."

I showed him the picture.

"Can't you see I'm not in the mood to talk?"

"You were the one who brought it up," I said.

"I did?"

"Mrs. Mooney in 'The Boarding House.'"

"That's different. That's fiction."

I told him that Joyce's fiction was heavily influenced by lived experience. Writing provided a way of dealing with everything that had gone wrong in his life. Although his parents were initially well off, his father's failure in everything he tried – the distillery business, politics, tax collecting – led to the family's downward slide. Joyce was withdrawn from private school and the family moved to increasingly less fashionable neighbourhoods, ending up in the north of Dublin. While Joyce won a scholarship to Belvedere College, he was never allowed to forget his precarious status. Thumbing his nose at social conventions, he fell in love with a chambermaid, Nora Barnacle, and the couple left for the continent so Joyce could concentrate on writing.

But poverty, depression, bad health and excessive drinking put him in the hospital, where he actually did some of his best work.

Faced with countless rejections, the publication of *Dubliners* was delayed by nine years. Meanwhile, his memoir *Stephen Hero* fared no better.

Once he finally was published, his was a solitary life marked by attacks from readers and critics (*Ulysses* was even suppressed by censors), meager rewards and belated recognitions.

As I thought about my own prospects, my eyes filled with tears.

"He was an outsider," Daddy said.

I nodded. "The oddball characters he depicts across the lower and middle classes are observed from the perspective of someone who doesn't know where he fits in. That's what makes his writing interesting."

But Daddy's thoughts were elsewhere. "Like Joyce's dad, Kaz was terrible with money."

"I thought he was an accountant," I said.

"No, he was just a bookkeeper. Even that he quit."

"Why did he quit?"

"He was the kind of guy who failed at everything. Flunked the entrance exam for med school. Dropped out of dental school. He couldn't even make it running a shop that made ladies' clothes."

"Did he ever find his vocation?"

Daddy looked at me like I was a five-year-old. "Forget *vocation*. He gave up on trying to find anything. Including a paycheque."

I lapsed into silence, fear washing over me.

"Daddy, can we visit the house?"

"Why?" His cheeks hardened like the shell of a walnut.

"I'm curious about where you grew up."

"That house means nothing." He buried his face in the book.

Stalker, sicko and all the other things Daddy had called his father rushed through my mind. I thought about how Kaz had pulled up in front of Granny's house with a bunch of friends in tow. He was the kind of guy who needed other men to witness his exploits with the ladies, and afterwards maybe he'd brag about how far things had gone.

These scenes from my family's past, a jumble of images, were coming alive and mixing in my mind with fragments of *Dubliners*. Rather than trying to separate fact from fantasy, it was easier to just let my imagination go.

In another picture in the album, Kaz stands in the middle, tall and good-looking, his hair lifted off his forehead, an elegant wave. Granny is clasping his hand, her head cocked to the side, her rosebud lips barely visible above the fox stole. On the other side stands his younger brother, Haruki. His eyes are near-set and quizzical, squinting in the sun.

Something had happened between the two brothers. No one talked about it, but I couldn't forget the pinched look on Uncle Haruki's face the one time I'd met him. That was the summer I was ten; we'd gone to visit him in New Brunswick.

I remembered he had downy white hair and gentle cheeks – so it was strange to see that flash of anger on his face. Or grief. I wasn't sure.

"Leslie looks a lot like Kaz." His jaw quivered, his eyes misting over.

Daddy didn't say a word.

Maybe it was simply the fact that Haruki had been the good son, while Kaz had been the bad boy, drinking and womanizing from an early age. I'd heard from Aunt Tetsuko that Kaz had dated a jazz singer while he was still in high school and gotten into all kinds of trouble.

But it couldn't have been easy for him when Haruki got accepted at med school. He was doing what Kaz had been expected to do – carry on the family tradition.

The sacred family tradition.

Ever since childhood, I'd been hearing about how my great-grandfather was the first ever Japanese-Canadian doctor. People at the Japanese-Canadian Cultural Centre still ran up to me, telling me how he delivered their parents and bandaged up broken noses.

I didn't know much about Dr. Kozo Shimotakahara and everything I did know came from Granny, who was hardly a reliable source. She'd written articles for Japanese newsletters singing the praises of her illustrious father-in-law, who'd left Japan at age fourteen and taken a boat to Vancouver, where he'd learned English from the ground up. It was a classic story of immigrant mythology, full of near-death escapes and larger-than-life adventures. Greatly exaggerated, no doubt. But he was revered by the community, and Kaz, I supposed, had always lived in his shadow – the screw-up, the degraded scion.

The days plodded on, each one more monotonous than the one before. To get out of the house, I went to the library, supposedly to continue writing my article on Faulkner.

"But we thought you were leaving academia," Mommy said.

I shrugged. What could I say? The lunches with my mother's friends had failed to spark enthusiasm for anything. Part of me was thinking I might as well just stick with the devil I knew.

But it was useless. I'd written practically nothing. I couldn't focus. I would stare at the computer screen for hours, editing the same paragraphs over and over again.

Walking past a garbage bin, I had an urge to dump my file folders and laptop in with the half-eaten pizza slices.

Most days, I ended up reading books that had nothing to do with the damn article. I'd even started rereading *Dubliners*.

Normally while reading, I'd gotten into the habit of drafting lectures in my head, so I'd be constantly looking for instances of "epiphany" and "modernist disillusionment" to explain to students. These days, however, I found that academic voice fading away and it was a blissful silence. For the first time in years, I could read without puzzling over what each sentence *meant* and simply let the words unfold, luxuriating in their sound and rhythm.

The more I let myself, the more I liked this childlike way of reading. I didn't give a rat's ass about epiphany. I had other things on my mind.

"Daddy, if you had to compare Kaz to one character in *Dubliners*, who would he be?"

"That's a strange question," he said.

"Well, we crazy professors ask strange questions. It's expected."

"Little Chandler. Kaz was always comparing himself to other men, and then he'd fly into these jealous fits. He always wanted what he couldn't have. That's Little Chandler in a nutshell, isn't it?"

I nodded, although the comparison threw me off. I'd pictured Kaz as a big, blustery fellow, full of bravado. He was the kind of guy who always had a lot of pretty girls hanging around him and knew where to find a cool bar. But now my image of him shifted, and I sensed that beneath his sparkler personality lurked a smaller, insecure man. The kind of man who's watching life pass him by, simmering in boredom and his own powerlessness. Until one day he snaps.

Daddy ran his hands through his hair, his forehead sweating. "On second thought, I'd say Gabriel Conway in 'The Dead.' Kaz could get very paranoid at times."

"Paranoid about what?"

Daddy's face reddened. "The same thing that made Gabriel crazy."

"He thought some old lover lurked in Granny's past?"

We all know what it feels like to be in a relationship that's going downhill and there's nothing you can do to stop it. Poor Gabriel. His marriage has been languishing for years, yet he deludes himself that his wife still loves him and it's not too late to reignite their passion. But as he watches her across the room at a Christmas party, his lust mounting with every second, her mind's on another man, an old flame.

How I could relate to her misery. That was how I felt every time I looked across the table and saw Bobby or whomever – and all that mattered was that I wasn't with the one guy I was meant for. Josh. It was hard to admit, but after all these years, Josh was the one who lingered on in my imagination.

"Gabriel wasn't paranoid," I said. "Gretta really was in love with another man."

Daddy looked shaken. "Maybe Mom was, too."

"What do you mean?"

Daddy rubbed his temples and flipped on the TV. It was clear that he didn't want to talk about it and I wasn't going to get anywhere by watching the infomercials.

The future stretched out like a sludge-filled pool. My head was pounding and all the furniture in my bedroom appeared backlit by a harsh light.

The price of last night's shenanigans.

I wandered downstairs into the kitchen.

"You were out pretty late last night," Daddy said, holding my gaze.

"When you came in, you set off the house alarm."

"Yeah, uh, I met up with a bunch of old friends from high school."

I could tell what was going through my dad's head: *bars do not stay open until six in the morning.*

I paced around from cupboard to cupboard looking for something to quell the gnawing in my stomach. How dare he look at me like that? Where did he get off? I rifled through a cupboard – finding nothing but Ovaltine – and banged the door. Finally, I poured a tumbler full of diet Coke and threw in a couple spoonfuls of instant coffee, a trusty eye-opener from high-school days.

Last night, Grant had invited me over for drinks. Actually, we'd been hanging out quite a bit the past couple weeks. I knew it was just because his girlfriend was out of town, but that was okay – with Grant, there was never any need to overthink things. I'd met him at the wedding of a mutual friend a few years back. When he looked at me across the ballroom, his eyes bulged, and I remembered thinking, So that's what Freud meant by *scopophilia.*

Both of us were always in relationships on the verge of dying or in the process of coming out of bad relationships. Which kept things safe and clear-cut.

Whenever I would visit Toronto, we would meet for drinks, which quickly turned into a glorious binge reminiscent of high-school drinking. Then, we would wake up the next morning and smile at each other sheepishly, the carpet a mess of condom wrappers, spilt drinks, scarves, masks and fake swords, among other accoutrements of historical costumes.

Last night, I'd arrived at his house in the Annex around eight. Tall, lanky, with cool blue eyes and an aquiline nose, he looked exactly as I remembered, right down to the oversized blue shirt smelling heavily of cigarette smoke. He greeted me at the door with a big, lush kiss, martini shaker already in hand. I remembered glancing at my watch at 9:07, and being acutely aware that it felt perfectly natural to laugh hysterically at his self-deprecating jokes – they all seemed to come back to his dyslexia, which, might I add, hadn't prevented him from making a killing in the real estate business – and my own life suddenly seemed quite hilarious and worthy of self-deprecation, too. The alarm clock said 10:11 when he pushed me onto his Egyptian cotton sheets, clawed his hands through my hair, and whispered, "Pretend I'm a bandit during the Norman conquest of England." Meanwhile, I was drifting back and forth between sheer sensations and musings about whether Lily Bart would be so hung up on sexual propriety if she were alive now. In the scene of her undoing, she makes an unwise decision to visit Gus Trenor late at night – lured to his home on the pretense of discussing an investment – and barely escapes being seduced/violated/raped. Readers differ widely on their interpretation of the sexual dynamics of the scene, but the key point is that Lily is socially ruined regardless.

(Yet there was something sexy about her ruination. . . . Maybe I wanted to be ruined, too.)

Before I knew it, a soft orange glow was peeking through the curtains, and Grant was shaking my shoulders. The clock said 5:44. He was saying that I had to go, because he had to prepare for a breakfast meeting. I rubbed the sand out of my eyes and explored the floor for my bra.

I'd wanted to feel like shit, and I did.

A few days later, Daddy and I were driving to St. Lawrence Market. In the traffic, I drifted off.

I woke up to a talk show blaring on the radio. I blinked. The market was nowhere to be seen. A dingy strip of Bloor ran past the car windows. Yellow signs of Caribbean restaurants, a Goodwill, a wig shop. The dark blockaded front of the House of Lancaster Gentlemen's Club, looking like a mausoleum.

"Where are we?"

"Lansdowne, my old neighbourhood," Daddy said.

"I thought you didn't want to come."

Daddy parked the car. "Want to get out and walk around?"

Heads draped in tinsel-shot scarves floated by. Men with jutting bellies swaggered past. I bumped into a shoulder and a face spun around, scrunching up like a bulldog and swearing at me in some language. But beneath the show of arrogance: a small, hard kernel of disappointment. I could see it glowing through the lines etched into his face.

Daddy was gazing down the street at a veiled woman holding a little boy's hand. The child pulled his mother forward with the pent-up energy of a puppy.

We turned onto St. Clarens. The houses had a pieced-together appearance: scraps of brick veneer, cheap siding and wrought-iron railings were stuck onto the bungalows, according to no apparent design.

"Has the neighbourhood changed much?"

"Back then, it was full of German and Chinese immigrants, whom Kaz didn't like. Now, it's full of other people he'd like even less."

What memories were coming back to him? Kaz stumbling down the street, tripping on the sidewalk? Laughing into the empty air?

Daddy paused in front of a three-storey brick house. It had a large porch, from which the paint was peeling like a sunburn. In its centre sat a flowered sofa, surrounded by beat-up bicycles and bins overflowing with cans.

"Here it is," he said. "The upper floors were for the boarders and we had the apartment on the first floor."

"Did Kaz sit on the porch?"

Daddy shook his head. "After he went crazy, all everyone wanted was for him to stay inside the house."

"The family had such high expectations."

Daddy glared at the ground. "Oh, *come on*. He was the doctor's son – he was given everything. The more he screwed up, the more his mother coddled him. She bought him a car. She put the down payment on this house."

It wasn't the first time I'd heard that Kaz had had it too easy. The Shimotakaharas were one of the few families that still had money after the war, because Dr. Shimo never lost his property. The government needed him and the few other Japanese-Canadian doctors to provide medical services in the camps. And in exchange, no one in their families was interned. They were the lucky ones, compared to other families like my mother's, who had lost everything.

Daddy led me down a muddy driveway. It dawned on me that we were trespassing when I saw the "Beware of Dog" sign attached to the wire fence.

My eyes travelled down to a small window sunk into the ground. The glass was streaked with grime and the air looked murky as an abandoned aquarium.

"That's where Kaz used to drink. He used to hide his whiskey bottles in the basement."

"It looks horrible."

"Funnily, Kaz seemed happiest there. He'd get out his guitar and start singing. *Blue Moon* was his favourite."

Too bad he'd never thought about becoming a musician, but of course the family wouldn't have approved. Looking at the window turned my stomach. I felt like I was trapped in that dark space, swimming through the damp, dusty air.

I thought about Granny standing at the top of the staircase and I imagined what she would have looked like, listening to his music. She would have still been quite young, though her beauty had probably started to fade. I could picture the worry lines coming in around her mouth, the corners of her eyes crinkling when she smiled, and I saw her beauty taking on another dimension, in the same way that dying flowers can look more interesting than flowers fresh from the florist. Perhaps she stood there for a long time, anxiously fingering the folds of her skirt, uncertain of whether to go down, unsure of Kaz's unpredictable moods. So she just stood there in the dark, still as the night, listening to the muffled music of this man she had married. This drunk, this stranger, this lunatic.

Like Gabriel Conway contemplating Gretta, I pictured Granny as a woman in a painting. She was a symbol of the secrets and mysteries that had always veiled my family's past.

"What are you doing here?" a voice said, jarring me from my fantasy.

The woman was speaking to us through the window. Her curlers bobbed, grey spools of thread.

"I used to live here," Daddy said. He explained that his grandmother had bought the house back in the early '50s.

The woman's cheeks lit up. "Mrs. Shimo. I remember my father talked about dealing with her. He said she drove a hard bargain." She looked at us with interest, introduced herself as Tina Poulakos, and insisted we come inside.

The front hallway was cramped, full of coats. The smell of grease and fried garlic had seeped into the carpet. Mrs. Poulakos led us into a living room dwarfed by large maroon sofas, covered in plastic wrap; the house filled me with a terrible claustrophobia.

Mrs. Poulakos was proud that her father had turned the boarders' quarters into nice, two-bedroom apartments. But the problem was that the area didn't attract families who could pay the rent.

Daddy snuck up behind me and pointed at a light socket with his foot. His tone was soft and conspiratorial, as he said, "I used to stick Wendy's fingers in that socket – boy, did she ever scream at the shock."

Granny had once told me that Daddy had been a rambunctious kid. He'd worn his father out, was the way she'd put it. Mommy had said that was typical of her to make light of his childhood, to sweep everything under the carpet.

As Mrs. Poulakos showed us around, I found myself imagining Kaz in various stages of decline. Staggering around the house, bumping into furniture. Passed out on the sofa. Bundled up in a rocking chair, his face ashen. I felt like the boy in "The Sisters," haunted by the memory of Father Flynn, his heavy grey face looming over everything like a ghost.

I knew that Granny had worked as a receptionist at an engraving company, and it occurred to me that she must have taken the job to support the family, to compensate for Kaz's decline. I pictured her high heels softly clicking down the hallway. She leaned toward the mirror and applied lipstick, the early morning sun filtering through the bay window, careful not to disturb Kaz. But Kaz would have been jealous – the thought of his beautiful wife being around other men all day must have made him livid. Paranoid fantasies of some hanky-panky with her boss probably consumed his mind. I could hear him confronting her when she came home late, after a long day, and I saw him blocking her way to the kitchen, his face blurred with rage.

"Where did Kaz die?" I was standing in the doorway of a cramped bedroom, the smooth white bedspread stretching out over the bed. "Is this where he lay after his stroke?"

Daddy's eyes twitched like he'd been given a shock. He opened his mouth and slowly closed it. After a moment, he headed for the front door.

We stood on the front porch saying nothing, while I watched his bewildered expression from the corner of my eye. The memory of Kaz lying in that bed, sick and vulnerable, must have been too much. But I sensed it was more than that. There was something about his death that left a horrible bilious taste all over my tongue.

"Let's get out of here," Daddy whispered.

We said our goodbyes to Mrs. Poulakos and walked to Bloor in silence.

chapter four

His wife was crying, and he felt nothing; only each time she sobbed in this profound, this silent, this hopeless way, he descended another step into the pit.

-Virginia Woolf, *Mrs. Dalloway*

"Congrats!" read the subject line. That was it. The email contained nothing more than Josh's signature, above the name of some swanky law firm on Lexington Avenue.

So he had made it. The "Congrats!" wasn't really directed at me. He knew that I'd become an English professor in a town so tiny there was only one theatre and the movie changed once a month. Meanwhile, he was quaffing an espresso on Lexington Avenue. "Congrats," indeed.

It gave me the creeps to picture Josh sitting at his computer late at night, in boxers and a dingy wife beater, a glass of cognac in one hand, googling my name with the other. He'd relish sifting through the evidence. I hated how the Internet left a trace of my every move. I couldn't even give a paper at a conference without the whole world knowing it was on "Deviant Sexualities in Modernist Fiction" or "Postmodern Apocalypse."

I felt like someone was watching me right now. Pulling my bathrobe closer, I stared out at the filmy grey sky, at the half-open Venetian blinds of the house across the street. Was that a flicker of movement, lit by the soft light of a computer?

"Congrats to you, too!" I typed.

Immediately, I got a reply: "Can we talk? There's something I need to tell you."

Sweat dotted my forehead, migrating to my armpits. If I didn't respond, he would think I was blowing him off.

"OK," I typed.

I forgot to include my new cell number. Then I remembered it was in my signature. Whatever. For all I cared, he'd forget to call. Better that way. Maybe we wouldn't communicate for another seven years.

"For they might be parted for hundreds of years, she and Peter; she never wrote a letter and his were dry as sticks; but suddenly it would come over her, If he were with me now what would he say?"

I put down *Mrs. Dalloway* and blew my nose.

I had assigned it to my father – somewhat maliciously, I'll admit. What man wants to read a novel that dissects the minutiae of everyday life, leading up to the climax of a dinner party? But I loved the novel and wanted to reread it, and since Daddy had been annoying me, it only seemed fair.

Josh had always reminded me of Peter Walsh, Clarissa Dalloway's childhood sweetheart. These guys shared the same spirit of adventurousness. Had Josh been a British gentleman, like Peter, he would be the first to head to India for the empire's last hurrah. They were eccentrics who loved their travels and sword collections and foreign women. They had larger-than-life personalities that splashed into conversations at parties, made outrageous claims, got everyone riled up, started fights, and then at the height of it all, slipped out the back door.

Years ago, when I was reading *Mrs. Dalloway* for the first time, I'd told Josh that he reminded me of Peter. He eagerly began reading it. But the depiction left him incensed. "I'm like that? Is this your way of saying I'm not going to get the girl?"

Later, after we'd broken up for the zillionth (but final) time, I'd feared that the comparison had been my way of predicting that we wouldn't end up together. Had I known it in my gut all along?

I remembered the heaviness that overtook my entire body the week of our first breakup. It was May, the end of the school year. Daddy came to get me and I slouched down in the backseat of his SUV, the weight of my earrings pulling at my earlobes. Montreal vanished through the rear window, with all its shabby elegant brownstones, overflowing recycling bins, *dépanneur* wine.

I didn't want to talk to Josh. So why did I keep checking my phone for missed calls?

We had nothing to say. We weren't together. There was nothing to say.

Life went on. I emailed back and forth with my department head, assuring him that my research was on track, even though I hadn't written a thing in days. I'd given up lugging my laptop to the library. My pile of folders had toppled over on my desk, spewing notes and fluorescent sticky papers everywhere.

I got an email from Ben Jameson, a prof in the history department, my only real friend in that town. We were both part of the transient pool of outsiders. After gravitating to each other at an arts faculty meeting, we'd commiserated over a few good beers and formed a kind of urbanite survivors' colony.

Ben wanted to know if I was still interested in sharing an apartment with him next year. It was a plan we'd hatched to preserve our sanity. The plan was that we'd share a dirt-cheap apartment in Antigonish during the week, but escape to Halifax every weekend, where we'd have our real homes. Since neither of us had to teach on Fridays, every weekend would be a long weekend, making the two-and-a-half-hour commute worthwhile, maybe.

At least Halifax was a city. I could see my therapist every week.

I responded to Ben that I'd think about it, if I decided to jump on the hamster wheel for another year.

A big if. Ugh. The clock was ticking.

I read and reread my favourite passages of *Mrs. Dalloway*, getting lost in the beautiful weather of St. James's Park, Clarissa's keen attention to the rustle of every blade of grass and the little stranger in a pink coat, and Peter's stubborn unwillingness to open himself up to the world of feelings. . . .

Of course it never took long for my thoughts to drift to our endless banter, our silly fights about Josh's misinterpretation of a novel, the drunken cruel words. He'd even nicknamed me "The Mean Girl," like we were back in kindergarten or something.

Maybe he was right that I'd willed the worst. Back then, I idealized tragedy. Turbulence in love had seemed so much more interesting than a solid relationship. It had taken me a while to come around to craving the latter.

Granny was released from the hospital and settled back in her nursing home. But she was sleeping fitfully, her eyelids clenched, her right arm shaking and rising as if possessed.

When Daddy came back from his weekend visits, he always looked drained.

"Any improvement?" I asked.

"Not really. The doctors don't know what the hell's wrong."

I wanted to hug him, but he looked so wound up, coiled around a hot kernel of anger. So I stayed put on the sofa, a book frozen in my lap.

"Wendy goes twice a week to visit. It's crazy." But beneath the show of disdain was a wellspring of guilt. He worried he wasn't doing enough, even though what he was doing was just about killing him.

One evening he returned late, looking near-comatose. "Four hours in traffic." He sat down at the table and stared at the broccoli and chicken.

"Do you want me to heat it up?" Mommy asked.

"I can't eat."

"Do you want a drink?"

He shook his head. "The operation didn't work."

In a leaden voice, he recounted what the doctor had told him. The very same vascular problem that had besieged Granny's left leg was now attacking her right. But the doctor wouldn't recommend another amputation, since the anesthetic would likely kill her. Besides, it wouldn't be long before the poison welled up in another limb.

At this rate, her body would be hacked to pieces.

What was going on in my father's head? The look on his face was a cryptic mix of horror and resignation. He picked at the crust of a dinner roll, chewing the morsel for a long time, as if he'd forgotten how to swallow. I watched his Adam's apple bob in and out, and it pained me to think that one day I could be faced with making a similar decision about him.

I thought about Virginia Woolf and her lifelong meditation on the connection between the body and the brain – a question no doctor could answer, she insisted. My mind drifted to her diaries and memoirs and I was thinking about how she often described her state of mind as "apprehensive." Ever since her mother's death, when Woolf was barely a teenager, she'd been prone to spells of depression and interminable headaches and backaches and breakdowns that, had she been alive now, would probably win her the label manic-depressive. Five times she tried to kill herself.

I had a vague memory of overhearing that Granny's mother had died when she was young, and I wondered if her apprehensive state could be traced back to her mother's absence. Or had her mother died? I couldn't quite remember the story. . . . Mommy's and Aunt Tetsuko's voices had been hushed when they were talking, a hint of scandal under their breath.

When I was a kid, I'd been afraid to visit Granny, because it freaked me out how her face would become a mass of twitches whenever I tried to hug her and I could feel her pulse racing through her dress. Often she was very thin and hardly ate. She just sat in front of her plate, chewing the same morsel for a long time, staring out into space, like she'd forgotten I was there.

It occurred to me now that perhaps her odd behaviour was due to having grown up without a mother. Terrible things happened to girls without mothers.

Woolf had been abused by her older half-brother, Gerald Duckworth, who used to buy her expensive dresses and take her on vacation, affecting a paternal interest, all the while behind closed doors calling her his "beloved" and fondling her breasts, as she recounts in her diary. I wondered to what extent her childhood violation was responsible for her turn to women – the excitement of kisses and caresses by her sister and other women, who were always more than companions. The amorphous, androgynous ideals embraced by Woolf and the Bloomsbury coterie spoke to how one's love life could respond creatively, resiliently, to an initial hurt.

Granny didn't strike me as the kind of woman who would have kept a diary, but if she had, I wondered what it would reveal. Would it explain the strange woman she'd become? Would it yield insight into her traumatized soul?

Daddy looked so sad and distant I wanted to jostle him from his thoughts. "What do you think of Granny's doctors?"

"I hate doctors. They don't tell you anything."

"Still," I said, "I bet they're better than Septimus's doctors."

Daddy smiled. "What does Dr. Holmes prescribe? A tablet of bromide and a game of golf?"

We began talking about Septimus Smith, the damaged war hero in *Mrs. Dalloway*. He returns from the First World War decorated in medals, but he feels like he's fallen out of the human race. His wife's sympathy and caresses fail to move him, and the more she suffers, the more he curls inward, curls into his own dark core. But Dr. Holmes insists that nothing's wrong with him – he's just in a funk.

The gardener comes in late at night and finds Septimus tearing up his writing and going berserk in the street. He's tortured by his own literary ambitions, which never amount to squat. Panic-stricken, Septimus puts down the pen and kills himself – a premonition of what's to come for Woolf.

"What's wrong with him?" Daddy asked. "What pushes Septimus over the edge?"

"Everyone in the novel is on the verge of going over the edge," I said.

Daddy nodded slowly. "Why are they all so desperate?"

While Woolf's mental state no doubt had something to do with it, it would be too easy to see the novel simply as a reflection of her own deranged mind. The context of the war offers a more interesting reading. Septimus's extreme apprehension and inability to connect with the world speak to a widespread sense of rupture felt by all characters in the wake of the war. They're all left reeling. Absent loved ones. Fragmented communities. No one looks at each other in quite the same way, even as "normal" life resumes. When I'd last taught this novel, I'd written an entire lecture that focussed on the single sentence: "The War was over, except for someone like Mrs. Foxcraft at the Embassy last night eating her heart out because that nice boy was killed and now the old Manor House must go to a cousin; or Lady Bexborough who opened a bazaar, with the telegram in her hand, John, her favourite, killed."

"Kaz was never the same after the war," Daddy said slowly. "At least that's what I've been told."

"What do you mean?"

"Aunt Tetsuko used to talk about Kaz before the war. He liked to swagger around at parties, talk big, buy drinks. He was this fireball of energy."

The black-and-white photo came back to me – his glowing smile, the debonair wave of his hair.

"So what happened?"

"World War II changed everything. Suddenly it was shameful to be Japanese-Canadian."

A stillness came over his face. I wanted to say something, but my tongue felt lifeless.

"Growing up," Daddy said, "I had no idea of the Japanese-Canadian internment. I didn't know why everyone in the family was so tense and miserable all the time. It was like walking on eggshells."

"When did you find out?"

He must have been ten or so, Daddy said. They'd gone on a trip to Montreal, where his grandfather was trying to reestablish his medical practice, since there was a demand for doctors there. At dinner, Dr. Shimo got drunk and started raving about how if it hadn't been for the war, his practice in Vancouver would still be thriving. How miserable he was that he'd been compelled to give up his practice and move to Kaslo to be the camp's doctor. The place had been bleak, nothing more than a ghost town. He yearned for the good old days of Japantown.

But Japantown no longer existed. It had been razed during the war.

Tears stung my eyes. I'd once visited the neighbourhood where Japantown used to be. It was nothing but a bunch of derelict rooming houses and boarded-up stores.

"Did Dr. Shimo ever manage to rebuild his practice?" I asked.

Daddy shook his head. "The Japanese-Canadian community no longer existed. Everyone was scattered after the war. No one had a need for a doctor who could speak Japanese, especially in Montreal."

"Did your parents miss Japantown, too?"

"Mom never talked about it. Kaz, on the other hand, would go on these rants. He'd be sitting out back of the house on St. Clarens, reminiscing about the old days. All his friends from back in the day – Jimmy Ennyu, Takashi, the Japantown gang. He thought he was a teenager again. There had been this jazz singer, Lily Edo, whom all the guys adored. Kaz dated her briefly, but she went back to Japan. Broke his heart."

"That must have been hard on Granny," I said.

Daddy shrugged. "She was off in her own world, too. It was around that time Kaz started hearing voices in his head."

"Voices?"

"He'd be wandering around the house and up and down St. Clarens, whiskey bottle in hand. Having conversations with people who weren't there."

In the midst of her breakdowns, Woolf had heard voices – she writes in her memoir about an obscene old man gasping and croaking and muttering senile indecencies, as she lies awake in bed.

Walking down St. Clarens, I'd felt that Daddy and I weren't alone, even though the street was perfectly empty. But it was inhabited by ghosts of a place that no longer existed. The voice of my crazy grandfather, and all the voices chattering in his head.

Late that night, unable to sleep, I emailed Josh: "Listen, there's something I need to set straight. Comparing you to Peter Walsh all those years ago wasn't my way of saying we wouldn't end up together. I was just confused."

I stared at the screen for ten minutes waiting for a response. Nada. Oh, well. Maybe he was asleep, even though it was only 2:08. He used to be a night owl.

So I sent Grant a text message: "If I were your prof, would you try to seduce me?"

Within two minutes, he wrote back: "Oh, baby, what I wouldn't do for an A. . . . "

Good old Grant. I could always count on him for a mood boost.

Suddenly, I wanted to see him and forget everything in the ocean of Grey Goose, but he was somewhere in Europe closing a deal.

***

A few days later, I went to the hospital with Daddy. I stood by Granny's bed, watching her sleep. A resident came over, and Daddy barraged him with questions. But all he would say was that he'd keep us posted, as he rocked on the heels of his gleaming runners.

There was something mysterious about the last trace of Granny's beauty – the dab of lipstick on her withered lips. Aunt Wendy must have come to visit that morning. She couldn't bear to see Granny looking pale.

Suddenly, her eyes sprang open.

Daddy hovered over her, peering in. "Mom, are you in pain?"

"I want to get out of this pose." She shifted a little, trapped in her dying body.

Daddy fiddled with the angle of her bed, but I couldn't help but read a more figurative meaning in her words.

I want to get out of this pose. At last, we were getting to the truth of her beauty. An uncomfortable, artificial pose. A glossy shell concealing secrets.

I got a text message from Josh: "Good. Peter Walsh is a wuss."

I smiled. That prick.

Five minutes later, another message: "Btw, something I need to tell you. Call later?"

That evening, Ted invited us for dinner. The house was the same as I remembered it from childhood – cramped, dusty, eerie. Heavy pine tables and faded braided rugs. All the furnishings had belonged to his first wife, aside from a few calligraphy scrolls and the Japanese doll.

While Mommy was in the kitchen helping with dinner, I wandered into the living room and examined the doll, leaning my nose against the glass case.

"What are you thinking?" Daddy snuck up behind.

"Just looking."

"You know you're going to inherit her soon."

She was beautiful, but I wasn't sure I'd want to wake up to her on my dresser.

"Where did Granny get her?"

Daddy told me that a man in Japan, who'd wanted to marry her, had given it to her when she was only seventeen. That was the year her parents sent her to Toyama in hopes that the matchmaker would find a rich husband. Three men had made offers, and one was the owner of a sake distillery – he'd showered Granny in presents. But then World War II broke out and if she were to stay in Japan, she would lose her American citizenship and be denied entry and maybe never see her family again. She returned to Oregon immediately.

"Why on earth would she come back?" I asked. "If the rich businessman had proposed, her life was set."

Daddy rolled his eyes. "By this point, she'd already met Kaz. He'd gotten his hooks into her. He must have been writing to her all year."

"Were they in love?"

"Who knows? Years later, when they were in the middle of a terrible fight, I remember Mom saying that she should have stayed in Japan."

"Maybe she was just saying that to torture Kaz."

I looked at the doll's careful detailing, her tiny fingernails and teeth. The teeth gave her an aggressive look – strange to see on such a delicate face.

"Wouldn't it have been considered unladylike to smile showing your teeth?"

"She's a kabuki dancer, a court entertainer. Who knows where women like that came from? Humble origins."

"Like Granny?"

"She was no Little Miss Innocent." Daddy grimaced. "She knew exactly what she was doing when she set her sights on becoming Mrs. Doctor."

"But didn't Kaz flunk the med school exam?"

"Still, Mom thought he'd at least become a dentist. He would bear the title of Dr."

"She must have been devastated when he lost his mind."

I didn't have any experience dealing with mental illness. Rezia, Septimus's wife, was flooding my mind with images. As he goes off the deep end, she's the one who bears the brunt of his breakdown. He feels nothing and withdraws from the world, having lost all capacity to feel, while her suffering becomes more desperate each day. That must have been what happened to Kaz, as he descended into the dark pit of his own mind, leaving Granny alone and bewildered. What a lonely thing to be the wife of a madman.

"Did Granny do anything to help Kaz?"

"She got him some pills. But there weren't a lot of psychiatrists in those days."

"Did the pills help?"

Daddy shook his head. "They made his craziness worse. But maybe that was because he kept popping them."

"What pushed Kaz over the edge in the first place?"

He just looked at me, his face closed like a chestnut. Something in my chest dislodged, surrounded by a soft burning. His glare made crystal clear that he didn't want to talk about it, but I was tired of being treated like a child. This was my heritage and gene pool and it affected me. I had a right to know.

I repeated the question.

Daddy wandered over to the bookshelf, his back to me. "His moods just flew out of control. Why? Who the hell knows? Bio-chemical imbalance, bad luck – take your pick. All I know is things had never been worse – he'd lost another job, he felt like a damn failure. More booze, more pills, more ranting about how his life was ruined. One day, he had a stroke. Then a couple years later, he had another stroke and died. End of story. A crummy ending to a crummy life."

The colours of the room – the burnt-orange curtains, the puke-green carpet – turned horribly vivid. There was a sharpness to his voice that went beyond anger and it stunned me to hear it directed at me.

Getting things out in the open was definitely not the way to go. I was all for good old-fashioned repression now. It kept things tidier and allowed damaged people to get on with their sorry lives.

In the distance, I could hear the rustlings of dinner, cartons of takeout being unpacked, the rise and fall of small talk.

"Dinner's almost ready," Mommy called.

I wanted to be immersed in that harmless, predictable noise.

It was late by the time we left. The highway poured on, a river lit by headlights. Mommy was lightly snoring in the front seat and I was pretending to sleep in the back to avoid an awkward silence with Daddy.

I watched him driving through my half-closed eyes, his shoulders hard as boulders. His jaw was so square, so tense, it reminded me of the skull of some prehistoric vulture. He kept his eyes on the road and sped ahead.

"Death was an attempt to communicate." This line from *Mrs. Dalloway* ran through my head over and over again.

I hadn't understood what Woolf meant when I first read it years ago, and I still didn't. Communicate what? At most, it seemed that death might be a failed attempt to communicate something.

Mrs. Dalloway has this revelation at her party when she overhears a conversation about Septimus's death. She's never met him. He's just gossip in her drawing room. Nevertheless, she reacts strongly – viscerally – to the news that this young man has thrown himself out a window. It feels for a split second as if her own body is being bruised, burned, impaled. And perversely, she wants nothing more than to feel the force of the ground hitting her, the thud against her brain. Suffocating blackness.

The eternal presence of insanity and death. Fear of going over the edge touches everyone. Is that what Woolf was getting at? The blackness is the same for us all in the end.

While chitchat and dinner parties leave Mrs. Dalloway dry (her own is a bit of a failure, really), the thought of Septimus's body hitting the ground moves her. The sense of identification with another's pain is somehow gratifying.

Yet as I reflected on Kaz's death and Granny's impending death, I couldn't honestly say I felt any such revelation. I didn't feel a connection or closeness to them for the mere fact of their dying.

Death was just a void. Death communicates . . . nothing.

Maybe I was skirting the issue. To understand Clarissa Dalloway, you have to confront the fact that she, like Septimus, wants to die. When she hears his story, she thinks to herself, *I, too, have the ability to throw it all away* . . . . There's a beauty to killing yourself on a whim.

I wondered if Woolf felt this excitement – playfulness, almost – in the minutes leading up to her own suicide. She was depressed. Again. Depressed and tormented by those wretched voices. Depressed by the reception of her writing in recent years and the onset of World War II. So she filled her pockets with stones and walked into the river near her house.

And yet, her suicide note to her husband reads like a love letter: *What I want to say is that I owe all the happiness of my life to you. . . . If anybody could have saved me it would have been you. . . .* There's a giddiness to her tone – she's leaving behind one lover to sink into the arms of another, and the anticipation is intoxicating. Death, the ultimate lover.

I loved reading Woolf's manic flights of fancy because they stirred up images and emotions in me. I thought back to my own darkest moments over the past year. Late at night, I would leave my office and make my way across the campus through the inky night air, and everything took on a surreal feeling, as though I were underwater, and after a while my feet went numb as I approached the empty highway leading back to my desolate apartment, and I'd think to myself, *This can't go on. I will go crazy if I have to do this for another year. I will kill myself if I have to do this for another ten years.* The headlights of passing cars and trucks took on a horrible beauty, washing me in light, and I imagined just letting myself go limp, like I were falling into a river, the Esso trucks coursing by.

But where Woolf presents suicide as something beautiful and liberating, the truth was that these stirrings scared me shitless. I recoiled. I ran home and slammed the door. I broke down sobbing on the floor, for hours. I loathed myself for feeling so desperate, so powerless.

I didn't want to die. I wanted my life to get better.

Maybe this was another way of death communicating.

The next evening, my phone rang while I was in line at Coffee Time.

"What's up, English prof?" Josh said.

A tsunami of anxiety hit my body. In five seconds flat, I was drowning in sweat, my pulse hammering.

Oblivious to my discomfort, he rambled on, filling me in on the past several years. Interning at the UN. Law school at NYU. Eighteen-hour workdays at the firm.

A dull ache filled my body.

"Your voice sounds different," I interrupted. "Raspy or something. Have you started smoking?"

He chuckled. "Naw, it's just that life's taken its toll on me. I'm getting old." His voice deepened into his imitation of a creepy old man. "Come hither, my little nymphet, get into the back of my van."

It was the voice that I used to call "Grandpapa Creepo." I couldn't believe he remembered after all these years.

The events of the last few days had left me frazzled, and his sicko sense of humour and puerile ways were pushing me onto shaky ground.

Still, I found myself wondering what he looked like. I wondered if his brown curls were turning salt-and-pepper and if his asymmetric nose still suited his face. I was curious whether the hairy patch on his chest would still have that sharp, metallic smell.

"So how are your folks? Is your dad still flying his planes?"

I choked on a laugh, or maybe it was a sob. It was funny that after all these years Josh would ask about Daddy, like he was still trying to impress my old man.

"So what are you teaching the kiddies these days?"

"Modernist fiction," I said, dabbing my nose. "The semester's over – I really don't want to talk about it."

"So the life of the mind isn't all it's cracked up to be?"

"I'm in no mood to talk about it. Maybe another time."

"So there'll be another time?" His voice sounded hopeful.

God, he knew how to press my buttons. Not three minutes into the conversation, and my eyes were already fogging.

"Well, baby," Josh said, "I could have told you a long time ago that you should say FU to academia. You're way too sexy for that cardigan and Birkenstock profession. You should have moved to New York a long time ago."

"Could have, should have, would have. Spare me 'The Road Not Taken.'"

"It's not a bad poem."

"I hate Robert Frost. There's a reason why he's taught in junior high."

"Look at you – so erudite and snobby."

"Oh, by the way, what was that thing you wanted to tell me?" I downed my coffee, hoping it would calm my nerves.

"On second thought, it's best if you just see it. I'll send you the link."

I clicked on the link and what opened was a page on the Student Union Bulletin Board – "The Worst Professor Ever."

"When I googled your name, this came up," read Josh's email.

Some kid, who went by "Activist" and signed all his postings with "Without Me, You'll Be Less Interesting," had started off the discussion: "Shimotakahara – English. I don't mean to harp on English professors, but it's similar to the prof noted above."

In the section above, my dear colleague Dave Howells was being lambasted: "Doesn't care about the students at all. Doesn't care if you show up or if you sleep through his whole class. I've seen students in the front row of his class playing PSP and he doesn't even give a damn."

Since when was it a professor's job to baby-sit and reprimand students? I hadn't been aware that my job description included singling students out with a "Young man, stand up and go to the principal's office!"

Moving on to Activist's gripe with me: "Things were fine for the first half of the year, but now she spends the majority of the class with an eerie silence hanging over the class, trying to spark some kind of discussion that obviously isn't coming."

To this, another learned soul, named "Rogue," had replied: "Agreed with this. Everyone looks down at their keyboards, hoping they're not picked on. . . . I've relegated myself to counting the number of times people say 'like' in their speech. Which class do you have with Shimo?"

And so the discussion continued. I couldn't bear to read any more.

What hurt the most was I knew it was true. Students did evade my glances, lost in the eerie silence. They sensed that I'd sunk into a deep depression, a big black pit. My pulse mounted like a drumbeat, culminating in a shower of tears.

It was the feeling of being the kid at school who forgets her gym clothes and has to do phys-ed in her underwear. It was on par with having to walk past the fence where all the cool older girls hung out. "Why does Leslie wear those prissy bows in her hair?" one would say. "Why does she walk like a penguin?" another would chime in. "Waddle, waddle."

Waiting in my inbox was another email from Josh: "Did you read it? I would recommend petitioning the dean to have the posting removed, since it's a university website and could damage your career. From a legal standpoint, there probably isn't much you can do."

Oh, so now he was providing me with legal counsel. Did I ask him to go on this dirt-finding mission? I slammed my laptop shut.

I curled up in bed and clung to a pillow. My life sucked. I was trapped in a hellish profession and I was never going to find an exit strategy. Worse yet, my misery was being broadcast on the World Wide Web.

Maybe this was how Kaz felt when he hit rock bottom.

Through the static in my brain, I faintly heard Daddy calling me to dinner. But I just couldn't bear to get up. I kept lying there, numb and sobbing. Images of Woolf's final moments danced before my eyes. Where was the closest river?

chapter five

The hollow of my hand was still ivory-full of Lolita – full of the feel of her
pre-adolescently incurved back, that ivory-smooth sliding sensation of her
skin through the thin frock that I had worked up and down while I held her.
                                                            -Vladimir Nabokov, *Lolita*

The waiting room was packed. I had no reason to be here. Yet here I was,
curled up in the corner of a plastic padded chair, my face buried behind a
back issue of *Glamour*.

Whenever I'd hit rock bottom, I would end up hanging out in a
hospital waiting room. I wasn't even sure how I'd gotten here. The last
thing I remembered was the humidity against my cheeks as I stormed out
of the house and just kept walking down Yonge Street and I didn't care I
was getting drenched in sweat and my toes were going numb – I just kept
walking. The next thing I knew I was standing in front of the grimy glass
doors leading into the orthopedic ward of Sick Kids hospital.

All too familiar memories were flooding back now, as I zoned out to
the sound of the intercom and watched the interns rushing past with their
clipboards and noose-like stethoscopes. Today, the place was packed with
kids with foot braces and immigrant families surrounded by fruit baskets

and other presents for the medical staff, like some sad attempt at Christmas. But I was scanning the crowd for prepubescent girls wearing baggy T-shirts and surly expressions. They were my tribe. Ah yes, here was one. A thin girl with stringy blonde hair, nibbling her thumb raw at five-second intervals. I knew how to spot them, based on the sweaty flush of their cheeks and their poker-straight posture, the telltale sign of a torso encased in cement, destined for the bottom of a river.

After I'd been diagnosed with scoliosis at age eleven, I'd retreated into the sanctuary of my mind and read books to hold on to my sanity. For two years, I had to wear an ugly fibreglass brace that wrapped like a corset around my torso and pushed my spine into the most awkward positions and gripped me so tightly that I developed breathing problems. While other girls were flirting with boys at the mall after school, I kept my head down and hurried home, wanting nothing more than to lie flat on the floor to alleviate the throbbing. To escape my life, I buried myself in book after book, imagining that I was immersed in the delightful company of Jane, Emma and Miss Marple.

An hour went by, and then another hour. The hopeful faces of the parents soured, as the kids got cranky. Still, I kept sitting there, waiting.

Waiting for what?

Waiting for nothing.

It was a pointless, masochistic ritual I engaged in whenever my world was spinning out of control. I couldn't stop myself from coming here any more than I could resist the exquisite pain of peeling off a dead cuticle.

The Worst Professor Ever.

I closed my eyes, the air conditioning washing over me. Memory fragments attached to every hyper-sanitized surface and blinding light were coming back, and it was strangely reassuring that these memories were immeasurably worse than the eerie silence that Activist had mocked. Nope, nothing Rogue could say could come close to how being here had hurt me. It was all coming back now – that horrible, still vivid feeling of being powerless on the exam table, as Dr. Martin Foote, a roly-poly man with white hair, ran his fingers, fat as hot dogs, along my torso and made a vice to manipulate my spine, until my whole body felt numb and tingling. And then I would have to stand up and bend over to touch my toes, while the good doctor stood behind me and again gripped my torso, prodding me, pushing me this way and that, testing the limits of my sapling bones. All the while, my arms were limp as a rag doll and I was staring down at the pearly pink flecks on my toenails, vestiges of our summer vacation in Maine, before I'd been diagnosed with anything.

Idiopathic scoliosis. It sounded terribly scientific, but really it was just a fancy way of saying that my spine curved like an S and no doctor had a clue why.

Idiopathic. Idiotic. Idiot.

Back in my bedroom, I peeled off my clothes and stood in front of the full-length mirror for a long time. After all these years, I was still mesmerized by my uneven hipbones and the peculiar asymmetry to my waistline, and the even stranger way my ribcage jutted out and dipped down lower on one side than the other.

My eyes migrated to the long, thin scar that cut diagonally across my torso like a seam, running from my belly button up to my shoulder blade. Over the years, the bright pink scar had faded to a ropey colour and texture. Twelve inches, Dr. Foote had told me, and I could still feel the dry skin on his doughy palms. Before the operation, he'd promised he would give me a beautiful scar – so beautiful I might even be able to wear a bikini eventually (as if that were my biggest problem). I remembered how cocky he'd been in talking about my body as if it were a blank canvas and he were a great artist brimming with inspiration, eager to cut across with his signature imprint.

That's a helluva scar, sweetie.

What happened to you? Samurai fight?

Can I touch it?

All the things old lovers and boyfriends had said to me over the years rushed through my mind, and I wondered if Dr. Foote had foreseen it all. Had he known that in marking my body, I would always feel this ironic detachment from my own flesh? Would I ever stop feeling controlled by him?

I wandered to my bookshelf and pulled down *Lolita*.

Why, you might ask, would I gravitate, now of all times, to this novel about the exquisite art of pedophilia? Nabokov's tale about a degraded old man defiling his pert young stepdaughter hardly seems the thing to cheer a person up. But nothing mattered to me since those students had maligned me – and the humiliation was doubly compounded by Josh's involvement – so I might as well just sink further into my masochistic mood. Just revel in it. I lay down on my bed and let my body go perfectly limp, sinking into the abyss of my own misery.

I stared at the cover for a long time: a close-up on a pair of pigeon-toed legs, clad in ankle socks and saddle shoes, slightly grubby around the toes. "The only convincing love story of our century," reads the endorsement by *Vanity Fair*. I'd heard this line before, and yet I'd never found anything terribly romantic or erotic about this novel. Fascinating, yes. Sexy, no. For me, it had always been a story about victimization and survival and a wily, foul-mouthed little girl struggling to hold on to some shred of self throughout her sordid predicament.

Humbert Humbert tries to control Lolita's body – cataloguing all her measurements, policing her diet, relishing in running his hand along the prepubescent slope of her spine. As she gets a bit older, the signs of her body maturing are the ultimate turn-off. He desires to freeze her as his perpetual lover-child, his "nymphet," forever smelling of grass stains and ice cream sundaes.

As I flipped through the pages, rereading my favourite sections, Humbert's hands turned into the probing hands of Dr. Foote, as he bent and moulded me, exploring the possibilities of my young body, testing the flexibility of my wayward bones.

I wanted to stop reading, yet I couldn't. The pain (and pleasure) of watching Lolita being violated was too immediate, too fascinating.

A couple days later, when I came down to breakfast, Daddy was flipping through the novel, which I'd left in the living room the night before.

"Did you know this book is ranked fourth on the Modern Library's list of the hundred best books of the twentieth century?" he said.

"Where did you read that?"

"Wikipedia." He sipped his coffee. "Is it really that good?"

I could tell by the way Daddy was looking at the cover with a mix of longing and fear that he wanted to read it. Like many readers, he associated *Lolita* with that irresistible combo of scandal, smut and literary sophistication, but he was probably worried that it was beyond him.

"Do you want to borrow it?" I asked. "I finished it last night."

"Oh, I don't know." He blushed.

"Come on. It's a riveting story of perversion and degraded family dynamics – who can resist that?"

"But it sounds so immoral. Why would I want to spend three hundred pages in the mind of a pedophile?"

"Oh, morals be damned." I flipped to the back of the book to Nabokov's Afterword and read aloud from the part where he explicitly states that "*Lolita* has no moral in tow. For me a work of fiction exists only insofar as it affords me what I shall bluntly call aesthetic bliss, that is a sense of being somehow, somewhere, connected with other states of being where art (curiosity, tenderness, kindness, ecstasy) is the norm."

"What does that even mean?" Daddy said.

"It means that literature doesn't have to be making a politically correct point. Criminals like Humbert Humbert can be given sympathetic traits that allow the reader to identify with him and explore states of mind beyond the ordinary."

Even as I was talking, however, I felt myself on shaky ground.

"Why would I want to identify with a pedophile?"

"Humbert Humbert isn't *just* a pedophile," I said. "He's also a lonely, wonderfully neurotic, poetic human being who shares some of the same anxieties and feelings as you and me."

"He does?"

Daddy's words echoed my own thoughts, and I wondered how I'd been pushed into the absurd position of defending this rascal.

And yet, I couldn't deny that I did feel an inkling of sympathy for him. Despite Humbert's obscene behaviour, what makes him bizarrely likable is the fact that he's painfully aware of his own monstrosities. He repeatedly condemns himself for what he's doing to his stepdaughter and he knows that his unhappiness and constant search for gratification have something to do with his career blues. Like me, he's a professor who admits to having turned to academe out of default. Back in his youth, he had dreams of being a poet, but the muse has left him cold. After two failed marriages – one of which culminated in a plan to murder his wife – he's sadly accepted his inability to connect with humanity, giving a poignant touch to his fall into depravity. And he wouldn't be the first academic to go this route.

I wondered if Humbert's cynical aloofness from his profession was at all connected to Nabokov's own experience teaching literature courses at Wellesley and Cornell in the 1940s and '50s, after he arrived in America, the Russian exile par excellence, his memories of his homeland forever marred by his father's assassination in the Bolshevik Revolution. It was amazing that Nabokov, while struggling with such demons, not to mention a full course load, found the energy to write *Lolita* in between butterfly-collecting expeditions – his other passion. Utterly exhausted, he would have burned the manuscript if his wife hadn't stopped him and convinced him to send it to some American publishers, all of whom promptly rejected it, scandalized by its smutty subject matter. After its publication by Olympia Press in Paris, the novel gradually won a cult following, but it would be years before Nabokov gained his literary due.

I thought about the loneliness of the writer's life and how my favourite writers liked to obsess over lost and illicit loves.

More than simply a story of pedophilia or academic disenchantment, *Lolita* elevates to epic proportions the quest for a vanishing love object. The death of Humbert's childhood sweetheart, Annabel, has left him with a void and insatiable hunger in his heart – he's tormented by flashbacks of his fumbling caresses and botched attempts at seducing the little girl who, in his mind, was destined to be his beloved. Following my latest brush with Josh, who could deny my own desire to turn back the clock? The early days of our relationship replayed in my mind, a montage of all the long walks we'd taken on the Plateau in Montreal, exploring the little cafés that sold the most delicious empanadas, standing in line together outside nightclubs in the middle of winter, me in a miniskirt – we were crazy to brave that slashing wind chill. . . . But most of all it was just the lazy afternoons at his place, as we lay on the sofa together and he'd be reading some book about how countries in Africa were getting screwed and I'd have some novel or other open on my chest, though I was more interested in covertly examining the downy blond fur covering his earlobes, cute as piglets.

It was my fault that I'd let our relationship flounder and die, all the while acting like I didn't even care. Like I was just watching myself in a movie. During our final breakup fight, Josh had accused me of preferring broken things simply because I found them more interesting, like half-dead flowers. He said I was twisted for sabotaging our relationship time and time again because I couldn't resist the suspense of what would happen next. I knew at some level he was onto something, and that incensed me, so I'd spat back that he was the sick one, he was the one who fetishized pain and perversion, he was the one who couldn't resist running his tongue along my scar.

"But if you didn't have the scar," he said, "I wouldn't love you any less."

But I didn't believe him. *Couldn't believe him.* It was as though I'd become so used to my life being a wreck, my body ruined, that I'd grown accustomed to assuming the worst and even revelling in a tragic ending. The more Josh and I bludgeoned our relationship, the more I'd romanticized it as my long-lost chance at happiness.

Why did I have this ass-backwards way of falling in love?

It dawned on me that perhaps it went back to that old conviction I'd long harboured in my gut: the best years of my youth had been stolen away from me, as I remained wedged between those fibreglass walls and later, lay helpless as a salmon fillet under the bright lights of the operating table. It must have been back then that I began fantasizing about being some other girl who was gloriously normal, who had a blond haloed head and ballerina-perfect posture and bleached white teeth. Those girls, whom I so desperately envied at school, were going off on first dates and learning to French-kiss and give hand jobs in parking lots to the boy next door. They were blessed with simple, idyllic relationships. That was what I'd been robbed of, thanks to my deformity.

Maybe this is what makes *Lolita* so appealing to readers. Humbert's diabolical behaviour fades into the background compared to his poignant sense of loss, his visceral belief that the only thing that really mattered was ripped away from him. Lolita and the other nymphets always appear as sepia-tinted shades fading away in his imagination. He doesn't understand why he desires what he desires and he's tormented by the absurdity and irrationality of his fantasy landscape, and isn't this part of the human experience? What reader can't relate to that?

Sometimes, when I'd get more anxious than ever, lost in the muddle of my own thoughts, I would find myself thinking about Art Lane. He always had a strangely calming effect.

Art Lane. My orthotist's name had been Art Lane. I remembered how his name lodged in my mind, conjuring an image of a lane full of hip galleries, windows illuminated by swatches of flesh-tone canvas and sculptures of primitive bodies.

He might have been an artist or musician at night. For some reason, I'd imagined that working at the hospital was only Art Lane's day job.

His nails were bitten to the quick, raw, fleshy nubs, and they smelled of cigarettes, or maybe the smell was coming from his long brown hair. Cigarettes suggested excitement to me – all the excitement of a louche, Bohemian life. And besides, he had an artist's touch, I thought at the time, as he placed the cold strips of gauze on my torso and used his fingertips to smooth them flat, and then patted me all over with his palms, warmth coming through the cold wetness. All the while, he was down on his knees, as he worked with the gauze and pail of water, his eyes parallel to my nipples, which were hardening through the wet undershirt and the sweep of this man's gaze. I wasn't exactly embarrassed. Fascinated was more like it. What was he thinking? He never said anything, as he made this mould of me, which he later would use to cast my brace.

But every so often, our eyes brushed and I detected a buttery softness. Like, even if he hadn't had to make a mould of me, he would still want to be touching me, exploring my subtle curves. It was just a flash, and then he'd look away, and I'd be back to staring at my toes, wiggling them to make sure I could still feel anything.

When I'd had my first set of X-rays taken, it had turned out that my curve was within the bounds of normal. Very few people, I was told, have perfectly straight spines.

"What's going to happen to me?" I asked.

"Nothing," Dr. Foote said, examining the X-ray, eerily lit up on the white screen. "We're just going to monitor you for the next while to see if the curve progresses."

"And if it does?"

"Don't worry about that."

"Because it won't?"

"We don't know, but don't worry. A pretty girl like you should spend her time worrying about getting the attention of the cute guy in your class." He chuckled and winked.

But how could I not worry? The image of my X-rayed spine, curving like the neck of a brontosaurus, haunted my dreams. A dull ache crept over my back and I found myself walking gingerly. My body felt damaged by some mysterious force of nature, possessed by demons, in need of exorcism.

Six months later, the curve had gotten worse. It was now at twenty-nine degrees. I peered at the new X-ray, across which Dr. Foote had drawn lines in white pencil. None of it meant anything to me, but I knew from geometry class what twenty-nine degrees looked like.

I couldn't be that crooked, could I?

I stared at my reflection in the exam room mirror, and for the first time I wasn't sure what I was seeing.

"Dr. Foote, I don't understand. You said I shouldn't worry, but look what's happening to me! *Why?*"

He said that during my growth spurt, one side of my vertebrae had grown faster than the other, causing my spine to buckle. But why one side of me was growing faster remained a mystery. Idiopathic.

"We have to take a more aggressive approach in treating you," Dr. Foote announced. "I see you've got braces on your teeth – a regular teenager."

Actually, I was only twelve, but I smiled at his lame attempt to make me feel normal.

"What we're going to do is similar to those train tracks on your teeth, except it'll be on your back."

"A back brace?" The bright lights seemed to flicker in time with my pulse.

Dr. Foote showed me a picture of a blonde girl smiling broadly, as she lifted her T-shirt to reveal the most hideous contraption that buckled in front. I jumped back against the exam table.

"What about exploring other options?" Mommy asked, her eyes going watery. "Physiotherapy, a chiropractor, reflexology. . . . "

Dr. Foote smiled sadly. "None of those treatments have been proven at all effective. Trust me, you don't want to take your chances with that New-Agey stuff."

"What's the success rate for the brace?" I asked.

"Sixty percent."

"What if I'm in the failed forty?"

"Then we pursue more aggressive measures. But don't worry about that."

Something cold crept around my stomach, but I had to know more. "And what is considered a successful outcome? Will I be perfectly straight?"

Dr. Foote's cheeks flushed and his upper lip began to sweat, like the downy skin of a peach. "My, my, you do ask a lot of questions." He looked over at Mommy. "What kind of grades does she get? I bet she's frighteningly intelligent."

"You don't know the half of it."

He chuckled and hugged his arms around his rotund body. "Well, Mother, perhaps you'll be so kind as to save me from our little Barbara Walters."

Mommy stared back without a hint of a smile. "Leslie has every right to ask questions. *It's her body.*"

Dr. Foote looked stunned.

Growing up I'd been taught that a girl should never let anyone touch her body – particularly if she didn't understand what was being done to her.

My cheeks were now slick with tears and sweat, as adrenalin gathered in my veins. "Dr. Foote, I want to be involved in the decision-making process, so if you don't mind explaining my options."

"My dear girl, there is *only one option* I could possibly advise." His pager went off and he rushed out the door.

I walked around the house examining our bookshelves, for lack of anything else to do. The ones in my bedroom were jam-packed, along with the shelves in the guest bedroom which doubled as Mommy's office. Over the years, several of her novels had migrated to my bookshelf and some of my old books had been ousted to hers, so Judith Krantz and Susan Howatch and Janette Turner Hospital sat next to my old L.M. Montgomery novels and *The Baby-sitters Club* series. I studied this hodgepodge with an anthropologist's fascination, as though these garage sale books held the clue to our old selves.

During those two years when my body was twisting out of control, I'd started "stealing" novels off my mother's shelf, and I remembered how they'd become my surrogate love life. While other girls were experimenting for real, I learned by reading that cum tastes like a raw egg mixed with detergent and women can get aroused by being dominated and treated roughly (so long as those cowboy hands are also capable of tender caresses) and all kinds of shenanigans are possible between step-siblings on historical estates. And at the higher end of the literary spectrum, women were generally ironic about sex. Forget orgasm, it's difficult to tell whether they feel much of anything. Flipping through *Bodily Harm*, I could remember how intrigued I'd been upon reading my first Margaret Atwood novel, and I paused at a passage I still remembered, where the heroine's lover tries to arouse her by saying, "Pretend I just came through the window. Pretend you're being raped," and she replies, "What's pretend about it?"

It's amazing how these women are so cool and blasé about sex. One figures it has something to do with the fact that they're unsure about what, exactly, they desire, thanks to the way their culture, their upbringing and patriarchy have rendered their desires cryptic even to them.

It was around this time that I first read *Lolita*, and I recalled being mesmerized by how our dear little nymphet takes ironic to a whole new level.

I found my copy lying open on the coffee table. Daddy was at the part where Humbert is driving Lolita home from summer camp and they have the most scintillating conversation:

"How was the hike? Did you have a marvelous time at the camp?"

"Uh-huh."

"Sorry to leave?"

"Un-un."

"Talk, Lo – don't grunt. Tell me something."

"What thing, Dad?" (she let the word expand with ironic deliberation).

"Any old thing."

"Okay, if I call you that?" (eyes slit at the road).

"Quite."

"It's a sketch, you know. When did you fall for my mummy?"

"Some day, Lo, you will understand many emotions and situations, such as for example the harmony, the beauty of spiritual relationship."

"Bah!" said the cynical nymphet.

Shallow lull in the dialogue, filled with some landscape.

"Look, Lo, at all those cows on that hillside."

"I think I'll vomit if I look at a cow again."

"You know, I missed you terribly, Lo."

"I did not. Fact I've been revoltingly unfaithful to you, but
it does not matter one bit, because you've stopped caring for me,
anyway. You drive much faster than my mummy, mister."
I slowed down from a blind seventy to a purblind fifty.
"Why do you think I have ceased caring for you, Lo?"
"Well, you haven't kissed me yet, have you?"

Lolita is the one who controls the flow of their conversation, disorienting poor Humbert with her irony and double meanings, enthralling him with her irreverence and sudden turns of speech. Although he's the seasoned older man, she doesn't hesitate to seize the role of seducer – no sooner has he slowed down the car than she's sucking on his face, treating him to the peppermint taste of her saliva. He can only guess at what's making her act in this delightfully lewd way – is it a girlish game to imitate a love scene in a movie? Is she about to recoil as his withered lips puncture through her fantasy? But, no, her sexual curiosity presses on, as she continues to captivate him (and the reader) with her wit and daring.

And so, perhaps it wasn't surprising that Lolita became my heroine during that turbulent period in my adolescence. Dr. Foote, Art Lane and all the specialists who ran their hands over my nubile flesh became, in my mind, a version of Humbert Humbert, and I was Lolita making faces and popping bubble gum and making sly remarks and asking probing questions that never failed to make them sweat. They were fascinated by me, they wanted to heal me, they loved me, and that was something to hold on to, even though I found them gross, intriguingly gross. Desire in a man's eyes was something to focus on, like the light at the end of a tunnel.

At least, this was how I would later remember that wretched period in my life. Maybe my therapist would say that to cope with the trauma, I eroticized the whole experience, or perhaps she would say that the story I've concocted is a means of repressing a deeper truth. She and I never talked about it, and I doubt we ever will. I prefer to keep my fantasies alive and fluid, and who can say how "real" anything was back then?

✳ ✳ ✳

Let me share another juvenile, decidedly unacademic reading habit that I'd managed to hold on to, despite the tiny letters at the end of my name. Whenever I would become immersed in a favourite novel, I couldn't help but believe that all other readers had exactly *my* experience of reading. Of course, I knew it was illogical – I'd taken seminars on Theories of Interpretation, and wasn't that what kept people in my profession in business anyway? Thanks to the endless proliferation of ways to read literature, we had something to peddle from school to school. And yet, I never bought any of it, not in my gut. If I truly fell in love with a novel, I believed in the most childlike way that there was only one world of the novel and it belonged to *my* imagination.

So during my walk down memory lane with *Lolita*, I'd assumed that Daddy was strolling by my side and having precisely the same experience of the text, as if he could telepathically read my thoughts and the novel was becoming this beautiful conduit through which he was gaining insight into why his daughter was such a screw-up. Everything I couldn't say to him was magically being conveyed without a word crossing my lips.

A couple days later, however, I discovered we weren't on the same page at all. Far from it. Instead of drawing him into my world, the novel had taken him on a journey into his own past. *My* suffering was the last thing on his mind.

Unable to sleep, I went into the basement and there was Daddy, stretched out in front of the TV. A film was playing. I immediately recognized it as Stanley Kubrick's *Lolita* – James Mason playing Humbert Humbert with just the right debonair creepiness, and Sue Lyons as our little starlet, her sexuality blooming yet tantalizingly muted to evade the 1960s censorship rules.

"I rented it," Daddy said. "The book was getting tedious. But the film's pretty good."

"You're not going to finish reading it?"

"Of course I'm going to finish it. I just have to get a sense of where the story's going."

Not a bad strategy. I often showed film clips in my classes to hold the students' attention.

I sunk into an armchair and watched Lolita prancing across the stage in her school play, a rhinestone tiara glittering atop her golden tresses. Oh yeah, I remembered this scene. It's toward the end, right before the big blowout between Lo and Humbert. By this point, his jealousy has reached such a peak that he won't even allow her to attend a party on opening night for fear she'll fall in love with a boy her own age. One has to sympathize with the poor girl as it becomes frighteningly clear that Humbert's desire and obsession always were a kind of sickness, and the only hope for her survival lies in escape.

"Granny was a beauty queen," Daddy said softly, the light of the TV reflecting off his face.

"I wonder if she got to wear a white dress and rhinestone crown like Lolita."

Daddy shook his head, a dreamy look coming over his face. "It was a Japanese-American pageant. She said she had to wear a kimono which couldn't be too tight or else the judges would take off marks, because the Japanese don't consider an hourglass figure beautiful. They like skinny and straight. The only revealing part of the kimono was supposed to be the dip around the nape of her neck."

"Granny told you all this?"

"I think so." Uncertainty clouded his face. "I couldn't have imagined all that, could I?"

"What do you think was on her mind back then?"

Daddy said nothing.

At last, he said, "I think she wanted to get away from her old man."

I sat there paralyzed, unsure of the implications of his words, and scared of finding out. Poor Granny. I didn't know what, but I sensed something horrible had happened that was destined to nip the bloom of her youth.

An eerie resemblance between the story on-screen and Granny's life crossed my mind. I shuddered and my feet went cold and clammy. It was one thing for Nabokov to elevate pedophilia to high art, and quite another thing for me to be confronted with the demons of my own family. (Or was it my own twisted mind that had become accustomed to finding the perversions of literature too close to home?)

Daddy and I watched the fight between Humbert and Lo escalate to hurricane proportions, replete with screaming, violence and shaking. And all the while, I saw a child version of Granny blotting out Lolita's blonde head, as though some computer-generated magic had gone to work on my last memory of her, stripping the years off Granny's face so she was restored to the pretty young mother in Daddy's photo album, and then further rejuvenated to the jewel of her girlhood, a touch of baby fat gracing her cheeks. So it was Granny as barely a teenager whom I saw flitting across the screen, her expression alive with the theatrical, self-conscious look, or repertoire of looks, that a girl who knows she's beautiful always has up her sleeve. And if push comes to shove, those looks can turn into weapons, or at least tools of deception. Lolita's great escape is enabled by her acting abilities. More important than simple beauty, her theatricality saves her in the end, and it was precisely that desperate theatricality that I now recognized in my memories of Granny over the years. It was as if she were constantly modelling herself on some half-baked impression of Greta Garbo or Rita Hayworth or maybe just the girl in the Maybelline ad. Whatever the case, Granny couldn't stop acting, perfecting her plastic smile, fluttering her lashes to high heaven, lying about her age, and I wondered for the first time if her histrionic behaviour had been learned young, very young, as a ploy to outwit her maniacal father. Like Lolita, had she long fantasized about getting away from her old man?

The movie was at the part where Humbert has absconded with Lolita yet again, and they're in the car driving through the desert to New Mexico. The camera focusses on his face at the wheel, while Lolita pokes up behind him in the back seat, and through the car windows loom the sand dunes, hazy and enveloping. Humbert's driving becomes increasingly erratic because he's caught sight of a dark car behind them and he's convinced they're being tailed by an FBI agent. But when he interrogates Lolita about a stranger she'd approached at the last service station, she replies, "What man?" Her all too innocent smile is clearly an act. "Oh, yes," she contrives to elude him again, "he asked me for a map. . . . " The car careens and comes to a grinding halt, due to a flat tire, yet Lolita's illusions and lies continue on, fanning Humbert's madness, while they stare at the car behind through the rearview mirror. We sense that Lolita is somehow in cahoots with the mysterious driver. . . . She has a hidden agenda, which her flashy smiles and tinsel laughter are just a means of concealing.

These traits of the small-time beauty queen and high-school actress had long flashed across my grandmother's face. Maybe she'd also been a little girl who grew up being accustomed to keeping a slew of dark secrets, implanted first by her crazy father and later her crazy husband, both of whom she wanted to get away from. It amazed me that she herself hadn't gone insane.

Somehow, her theatricality had saved her. She was a survivor, like Lo.

chapter six

"I've given you all the money I have." Tears glistened in her white-ringed eyes. "Can I buy you with my body?"

-Dashiell Hammett, *The Maltese Falcon*

Mommy found me with my head on the kitchen table. She stroked the back of my neck and murmured soft words, yet anxiety prickled through her fingertips.

It was already mid-July, and I'd figured out nothing. At this rate, I would have no choice but to return to Antigonowhere. For another whole year, I'd be forced to stand in front of the students' mocking stares.

I could hear them texting and tweeting already.

"Shimotakahara – English. I don't mean to harp on English professors, but when was the last time she got laid?"

"I know," Rogue would reply. "She's more sex-deprived and schizo than ever. I'd rather have Clytemnestra teach the class."

As if these kids would be familiar with Greek tragedy. My giggle turned into a shower of tears.

"What's wrong?" Mommy asked.

"I'm a complete failure. I deserve to be unhappy."

She shook her head and assured me that she could help. Once again, the plan began with a list. This time I was supposed to call all the people whom I had worked for outside academia. Summer jobs, internships, it didn't matter how small the gig. I needed to let them know that I was looking to find a "new application" for my "outstanding research and communication skills." Mommy was full of enthusiasm, but I could barely lift my head.

Since I'd only had two jobs before English literature took over my life, the list was short indeed.

The first name was Uncle Bill. Back in the '80s, he'd founded his own architecture studio and it had grown into a large, dynamic practice. The summer after I'd graduated from high school, I'd worked as their receptionist. Uncle Bill met me for lunch and was his usual charming, sarcastic self, but as soon as I suggested working for him again, a pained look crossed his face.

"With your brilliance, Leslie," he said, "won't you be bored doing clerical stuff? You're creative. You need to get out there." Something might be available down the road if I really got desperate, but he knew I could make it on my own.

Great. Another pep talk.

The second person was Ellen Powell, my boss during a summer internship at the Ontario Women's Directorate. Googling her name, I discovered she had left government and was now at an international development NGO. Much to my surprise, she was friendly in her email and wanted to meet. Showing me around her crowded office, Ellen still had the pertness of a canary and I wondered why I'd never followed her advice to study public policy. As I told her about my three useless degrees, she laughed and said, "You'll have to get over your self-deprecating air." Although her organization didn't have anything at the moment, she offered to meet me again once I'd moved back and share her contacts.

I left her office with a flutter in my chest, but as I walked along Yonge Street, the hope faded. A bright red "Help Wanted" sign caught my eye in the window of a lingerie shop. A grungy homeless man wended his way through the crowd and jumped in front of me, coffee cup in hand.

There was no assurance that anything would work out. I could move back and find myself standing at the end of an EI line.

Daddy was glad that I'd gotten off my butt, but he was a manager, used to managing for results. He wanted to know how I was making out, and whether I'd reached any decisions. He wanted status reports to gauge how my choices were going to affect his life. After all, if I sunk into a long period of depression, there wouldn't be enough room for both of us on the couch. Besides, he had his own crisis to deal with. Granny's ailing health and dementia were enough for him to handle – he didn't need a crazy daughter, too. After a couple more blowouts, he'd made it pretty clear that my line of credit was running thin. I wondered how long this could go on before our relationship degraded completely.

"Help me, Mr. Spade!" I read aloud. Daddy and I were sitting at the kitchen table. He was eating mac and cheese with wieners and I'd fixed myself a salad. Mommy was out to dinner with friends.

I continued reading from Brigid O'Shaughnessy's dialogue in *The Maltese Falcon:* "I haven't lived a good life. . . . I've been bad – worse than you could know – but I'm not all bad. Look at me, Mr. Spade. Look at me, Mr. Spade. You know I'm not all bad, don't you? You can see that, can't you? Then can't you trust me a little?" I fluttered my lashes and looked askance.

"I remember that scene from the movie," Daddy said. "Great movie. Humphrey Bogart played Sam Spade to a T. Very cold and wolfish."

"Like you."

Something about the way Hammett describes Spade's face as one big V – his chin a jutting V under the more flexible V of his mouth – reminded me of my old man.

I expected his face to fall, or at least show some sign of anger, but he appeared unfazed. Happy, even. He didn't mind one bit that I was calling a Spade a Spade.

Hammett is known for creating a new kind of detective who's mean and street smart, in sharp contrast to gentlemen detectives like Sherlock Holmes. Spade pulls no punches during investigations, even if the prime suspect is a beautiful, vulnerable woman. He has no problem looking her in the face and stripping away all her illusions and lies.

On more than one occasion, I'd seen Daddy barrage Granny until she was left a quivering mass of nerves. All the Christmas dinners and Sunday brunches, as I thought back, had had their sour moments that, if sour enough, just might set him off on one of his rampages.

"I'm looking forward to reading it," he said.

"You'll love it." It would be like looking in the mirror.

The next time I was at the DVD store, I rented *The Maltese Falcon*. I'd seen it twice before, but I wanted to see it again.

Daddy came into the basement just as I'd set myself up with a bowl of chips, and plopped down on the couch.

"Don't mind if I join you."

My shoulders were so tense with him beside me that I couldn't focus on the movie. But soon everything faded into the deep shadowy lighting and smoke-filled interiors I'd always loved about film noir.

A beautiful blonde who goes by the name "Miss Wunderly" – but later turns out to be Brigid O'Shaughnessy – seeks Spade's help. She's full of hysterical cries about how her sister has disappeared and maybe a thuggish boyfriend is at the heart of it all, but the twists of the plot fade into the background compared to this woman's sheer lying ability. As she paces around her hotel room in a silky striped robe that slinks over her stunning figure – wringing her hands, her face vacuous as a porcelain bowl, crying, "Help me, Mr. Spade!" – he's onto her wiles. The shadows of the Venetian blinds play over her body and you just know she can't be trusted.

There was something eerily familiar about this woman.

And then it hit me – she reminded me of Granny.

My earliest memories of Granny were of the time when her beauty was starting to fade, but even so, she remained a lovely woman. A little too vivacious for some people's taste. She wore low-cut dresses in splashy prints and fuchsia lipstick. It irked my father to no end that she didn't dress her age and obviously didn't want to be a grandmother, rarely coming to visit us. Apparently, she'd been just as vain when he was growing up. She loved nothing more than when men would mistake her as his older sister, giggling histrionically and leaning forward on the edge of her chair (he used to do a funny imitation).

Daddy pretended not to care, but after we'd seen her, he was always in a bad mood.

The more I watched Brigid's sidelong glances, the more I could relate to Daddy's desire to "investigate" Granny and pry open her secrets.

What was it about her that we found so fascinating? It was the same inscrutable quality that gave Brigid her allure. There's something intoxicating about the theatricality of these women, as if their bodies are simply an extension of their carefully styled hair and overly made-up lips, heightening the enigma of what lies beneath: Does she have feelings? Or is she just a gorgeous automaton? What motivates her to act?

I thought about how, when I'd first left home for university, the femme fatale had appeared the icon of sophisticated femininity. There was a repertory cinema in Montreal that played all the classics – *Double Indemnity, The Big Sleep, Gilda, The Lady from Shanghai*. Enthralled by Lauren Bacall's sultry, brooding stares and Barbara Stanwyck's agitated pacing in a cloud of smoke, I'd aspired to fashion myself into a woman of their ilk. I scoured the vintage shops for slinky, retro clothing in black, maroon and emerald green, and accented these outfits with rhinestone brooches and fishnet stockings and stiletto heels. My friend Sasha and I frequented artsy coffee shops and clandestine nightclubs, where we smoked long, thin cigarettes – bitch sticks, as Sasha called them – and exhaled in fast streams through our nostrils. When men approached us, we looked away, trying to appear mysterious, but we let them buy us martini after martini and the room soon took on a strange depth, as if through a wide-angle lens.

Sometimes I let these men seduce me, and I'd wake up in a hotel room or dingy apartment in an unfamiliar part of the city, an overflowing ashtray on the nightstand. I crept out, at five in the morning, my pulse hammering. Street names all in French, not a cab in sight. But, in a perverse way, I was enjoying myself – the sense of clandestine adventure, the risk, the thrill.

Why, you might wonder, was an intelligent girl like me doffing her breeches with strangers? Had you asked me at the time, I would have probably quoted from Foucault's *History of Sexuality*, which I'd just read for the first time, and according to my sophomoric, half-baked understanding of what Foucault was saying: *what was bourgeois monogamy except the ideology of the ruling class?*

How much more intriguing to explore the multiple points of resistance. Promiscuity took on a political dimension.

But in retrospect, the truth probably lay closer to home. After all those years of my body twisting out of control, after enduring an operation that left me with four vertebrae fused and a metal rod welded to my spine, I felt a curious detachment from my body. My extremities were always cold and tingling – my feet, hands, nose. I wiggled my toes and it surprised me they still had feeling. I put on lipstick and powdered my cheeks, but all the while I felt as though I wasn't looking at myself, I was looking at a mannequin or actress, and I was the director in some made-for-TV movie telling her what to do, what to feel. But she wasn't getting it; she just kept standing there. Lifeless, fakely smiling.

Some nights, I still dreamed about the mask covering my face while the nurse told me to slowly count backward from one hundred and the bright light was shining off her acne-marked skin, and that was the last thing I saw before my body became light, so light, as if it was almost weightless. I thought I must be dying and it surprised me I was so calm. It wasn't so bad, kind of beautiful actually.

But I hadn't died. I'd woken up a couple days later, my head full of cotton batting, my body one big wound. I expected to be in a body cast or something, I expected they'd at least bandage me up tightly, so I could just lie there, immobile, scabbing over, my bones stiffening for several months. Instead, two rosy-cheeked nurses were pulling me up and I was forced to stand behind a walker. I had to take a few steps, and then a few more steps, until the nausea and pain of skin ripping unsewn was too much. I crumpled to the floor like a marionette.

As I got older, men sensed an emotional emptiness in me and I could tell it excited them. There was a kind of power, I discovered, in feeling outside of my body; it freed me to play with my identity. One evening, I'd introduce myself as Julie, the next evening, Simone; an art history student one moment, a psych major the next. I loved lying about who I really was, but more than pure lying, I loved interspersing truth with fiction. While swirling a glass of wine, I'd suddenly find myself pouring my heart out to a complete stranger about how my surgeon had been an arrogant prick, or how I feared I'd never find my calling in life. The stranger smiled and drew closer. But in the next breath, I'd be telling lies.

Maybe that was why the femme fatale still fascinated me. She's a woman who doesn't know who she is – her past is nothing other than a looming question mark. Her search for distractions and the gratifications of sex and money are just a way of keeping the mystery of her tormented self at bay.

As I watched the shadowy scenes of the film unfold, it occurred to me that this mystery is far more compelling than the mystery of the Maltese Falcon itself. The Maltese Falcon is just a pawn; all the crooks and thieves in the story are trying to get their hands on the bejewelled bird, but in the end no one can have it. The bird slips away – it's "the stuff that dreams are made of," as Spade puts it – or is it just a cheap plot device, the perfect MacGuffin?

No, it wasn't the bird, it was the mystery of Brigid's troubled identity that kept me wanting to reread the novel and see the film one more time. A question the story never resolves. Who is this woman? What led her to a life of crime? All we know about her past is that she lived in Hong Kong, but what was she doing there in the first place? She simply appears a drifter who, for lack of any ties in America, ends up in the Orient, veiled in mystique. Her beautiful face is a screen onto which others project their dark fantasies.

Cherchez la femme. . . .

What threw a wrench in my "femme fatale" persona was that I fell in love with Josh.

We met during the fall semester of my second year at McGill. I noticed him staring at me when I walked into "Intro to East Asian Studies," which I'd decided to take on a whim – thinking it might help me gain insight into my motherland. That didn't happen, since the class focussed primarily on Chinese culture, but it wasn't a complete waste.

Josh was the guy always sitting in the front row, arguing with the poor prof about something or other. He took her on about the finer points of Said's theory of "Orientalism" and roundly condemned Dorothy Ko's feminist argument for the empowerment of women through the practice of Chinese footbinding. Often, it seemed he was arguing simply for the sake of arguing, but I had to admit the guy had a nimble mind. And he was kind of cute, too, with his head of wild curls. Unfortunately, he had a terrible fashion sense. Threadbare plaid shirts and silver runners and an even more outlandish silver briefcase.

So I never thought I'd fall in love with him, of course. We were just friends hanging out. First, he invited me to a screening of *Realm of the Senses*, and then we began watching films in his basement apartment on a regular basis (not all of which were as artsy and pornographic as *Realm*), and since we were both reading a good deal of psychoanalytic film theory, we never had any shortage of stuff to talk about. Long, boozy dinners followed – and Josh was an amazing cook.

Sometimes other friends of his would drop by to join us. I noticed he had a surprising number of attractive female friends, who, like me, didn't seem to be his girlfriend. They lounged on his sofa, showing off their long, bare legs and complaining about some relationship gone awry. We smiled at each other guardedly, clearly hoping the other would leave – but why? It wasn't like either of us was into Josh. So what was it that we found so enticing about this guy anyway?

Maybe it had something to do with his stories. He told a lot of funny, sad stories about his childhood, most of which centred around his hippy parents who'd given up all their worldly possessions to join a commune, where the children were only fed bananas. No joke. And mothers weren't allowed to pick up their babies when they cried – for fear that too much affection would breed tyrants – and breastfeeding was considered the ultimate sin.

I found it touching that if Josh so much as caught a whiff of bananas, he'd gag or run to the washroom, but he loved drinking milk. He quaffed chocolate milk by the litre.

The morning after we slept together, I woke up feeling like rigor mortis was setting into my neck. His futon was hard as rock. *Oh shit, I can't believe I slept with Josh.*

I sat up and surveyed the greasy popcorn bowl and empty bottle of Le Villageois on the floor in front of the TV and the crumpled blanket on the couch, where he'd started caressing my knee last night, like he hardly knew he was touching me, and I remembered his touch had sent soft tingles all over my back. I also had a hazy recollection of him reaching under my shirt, exploring my scar, kissing it, a peculiar mix of curiosity and tenderness crossing his eyes. Like he really felt my suffering. That look, that must have been what forced me to give in.

And then he was parting my thighs, burying his face, sending rippling sensations through my flesh with an intensity I'd never before known. I broke a sweat and my powder started to dissolve and he kissed the femme fatale lipstick right off my lips.

It was disarming and exciting and I knew I'd crossed over into some unknown territory where I couldn't be blasé, where I actually felt something vivid.

Before long, I was waking up most mornings in his apartment, my neck sore but the rest of my body purring.

Later, after we'd been dating a while, I accused him of planning to seduce me all along. There was a careful strategy to his seeming spontaneity. A wolf in sheep's clothing, I called him. He smiled, agreeing with the metaphor.

To my surprise, Daddy wasn't enjoying the novel. When I asked him about it, a sour look came over his face.

"I've put it down. I'm off reading for a while."

"Okay." Heat suffused my cheeks. "Do whatever you want."

He was back to flying his planes with a vengeance. Every morning, he'd leave the house at the crack of dawn and not return until dusk, sunburned and smelling of gasoline. At night, he was down in the basement working on his newest baby – a World War II fighter jet. Gluing together the wooden pieces and covering them in slick black plastic relaxed him in a way that books simply couldn't.

Reading stirred up feelings, icky feelings. His model planes allowed him to escape all that and block out people altogether. Out on the flying field, nothing existed beyond him, the plane and the empty sky.

He was most content in the world that Hammett created, a world not quite devoid of feelings, but a world where feelings and emotions certainly couldn't be trusted. Feelings were what made you play the sap.

I wondered if he wouldn't have been happier living out his days like Sam Spade, free of the responsibilities of family altogether. Considering what a drain I'd become, perhaps he'd come to regret having a kid at all.

Sometimes, when I was growing up, I would imagine that I had a brother. This phantom brother popped into my mind, particularly when my parents would be fighting and Mommy would retort, "I can't imagine how horrible you'd be if we'd had a son!"

I'd never understood Daddy's phobia of fathering a son, because most men wanted boys with whom they could play sports. A son would have taken far more interest in his model planes.

As I got older, I realized that his preference for a daughter rested on some pretty old-fashioned stereotypes. Daughters were supposed to be sweet, obedient and eager to please. Sons, on the other hand, were rebellious and stubborn and invariably clashed with their fathers.

At times of high tension, I would imagine the phantom brother having it out with Daddy. There would be screaming and violence culminating in a "Get out of the house!" Everything that was pent up in Daddy's chest – everything he couldn't say to his sweet little girl – would come out.

I wanted to have it out with him. For I wasn't his sweet little girl. I had my own dark moods and aspirations that didn't fit into his scheme of life.

There must have been a moment when Daddy and I began to grow distant. There must have been a day when we realized that our whole approaches to life were day and night. The more I thought about it, memories flooded back. One memory in particular.

The summer I was five and getting ready to enter Grade One, Mommy put Daddy in charge of teaching me to walk to school. Every weekend we practiced by trudging side by side through the August heat, and I could still remember how long the block to Yonge Street seemed, the sweat pooling on my cheeks by the time we got to the corner store. Sometimes Daddy would buy us a Sweet Marie to share and we'd silently nibble the nutty chocolatey mess for the remaining four blocks to Bedford Park Junior Public School.

These walks were one of the few times I could recall being alone with my father, just the two of us.

"What are you up to these days, Luby?" (For some reason, Daddy used to call me Luby. I had no idea how he'd come up with this weird nickname.)

"I just wrote a story called 'Donna and the Rainbow.'"

"About your mother?"

I nodded.

"When are you going to write a story about me?"

"Don't worry. I'll get to it."

I was excited that I was now considered capable of walking to school on my own – it was my first venture into the wide open world. Daddy kept quizzing me about where to turn left and right and became alarmed when I got the two confused, but in my mind the whole point wasn't to get to my destination so much as to enjoy the stroll and window shop and let my mind wander. The colours of everything appeared so much more vivid through my dreamy sense of independence.

Then the day of the test came.

Mommy was standing on the front porch watching me venture down the street by myself, while Daddy trailed a half block behind on his bicycle. I could tell that he felt proud about having taught me something and I wouldn't let him down – soon I'd be travelling all over the world. Images of Paris, New York and Rome, which I'd seen on TV, were passing before my eyes as I approached the corner.

"Where are you going, Leslie?"

I looked over my shoulder and Daddy had jumped off his bike, his cheeks reddening.

I'd turned the wrong way. Rather than heading toward my school, I was headed for the 401.

Mommy was stunned – couldn't Daddy teach me anything? And was I directionally impaired? Now they were going to have to hire an older girl to walk me to and from school.

It wouldn't be the first time I'd let my father down, and vice versa.

"That's just great," Daddy said.

The doctor had just told him they had to make a decision. Granny's remaining leg was in bad shape. If we were going to operate, the time to act was now.

We stood around her bed, while Daddy and Aunt Wendy debated the options. He was in favour of letting nature take its course, but Aunt Wendy didn't feel ready to hang a "Do Not Resuscitate" sign on Granny's bed. Her face crumpled. She wasn't ready to say goodbye.

Mommy took Aunt Wendy to the cafeteria, while Daddy and I stayed behind.

Granny's eyes were clenched and a weird noise was coming from her jaw. It was like shells were being ground up. I wondered if I did that, too. Often I would wake up with a deep ache permeating my teeth.

"What do you think she's dreaming about?" I asked.

"Her whole life must be running through her mind. Isn't that what's supposed to happen before you die?" Daddy laughed.

"No, seriously," I said.

He sat down and stared at the floor. "There were times when I could tell she was scheming. I bet those moments replay in her dreams."

"Scheming about what?"

"I don't know. Looking for an exit strategy, maybe. She always had a hidden agenda."

I thought of Brigid scheming to get her hands on the falcon and scheming to get Spade on her side – buying him with her body – and all the while, you never know what she's really up to. It chilled me to think of Granny as that kind of woman.

"What do you remember?"

"Listen to this," he said, pressing buttons on his digital recorder. "Last year, before her mind went funny, she told me some stuff about growing up in Portland."

I leaned forward.

His gaze softened and something crossed over in me. Despite our hostility, we smiled at each other warily.

The recording started to play. In the first section, Daddy wanted to know about the neighbourhood where the Japanese-Americans had lived in Portland and where her father's dry-cleaning business had been. He asked why it was named "Elk Cleaners." Granny couldn't answer, and Daddy was getting frustrated.

"This is where it gets really interesting," he said, turning up the volume.

He was asking about how her father had met her mother.

"He went to Japan to get a picture bride." Granny explained that picture brides were young Japanese women whose photos were circulated by the matchmaker to Japanese bachelors living in America. Once a bachelor had selected the women he wanted to meet, he would travel to Japan to make his choice.

"So your mother was a picture bride," Daddy said.

"Not exactly," Granny said.

Upon meeting his selection, Granny explained, her father found that the women weren't half as attractive in person. This led to a blowout with the matchmaker – he'd paid a hefty fee and travelled at great expense to Toyama.

Suddenly, his eyes lit up upon seeing the matchmaker's secretary in the corner.

"I'll take her," her father said, pointing. They married the next day.

"Was your mother pleased about this turn of events?" Daddy asked.

A long pause.

"I don't think she ever wanted to leave Japan," Granny said at last. "But my father promised her great riches. A big house full of servants. She didn't know he was just a dry cleaner."

Daddy laughed and pressed the stop button. "Pretty funny, don't you think?"

At last, we were getting to the truth about Granny's past. A shadowy image of her mother surfaced in my mind – a tiny woman with downcast eyes and a mysterious half-smile – I'd seen her in the black-and-white photo on Granny's wall. The femme fatale behind the femme fatale. Perhaps this woman was at once a gold digger and a poor innocent, duped into a life she'd never wanted. My pulse surged, as the past caught hold of my imagination, like a jolt of adrenalin, a drug.

"I want to hear more." I fingered the digital recorder, but Daddy grabbed it away.

"No, you've heard enough."

"Oh, *come on.*" My hands shook.

Now that he'd drawn me in, I was being shown my place. *He* was in control. I was just a sidekick to boss around and provide an audience.

A few days later, Daddy came home carrying a large glass case draped in tea towels.

"I got the doll," he said, as Mommy and I crowded around.

"But Granny isn't even dead yet."

He said he was worried that Granny's cousin, who collected Japanese art, might convince Granny to give her the doll.

"Fine. I never said I wanted it."

The doll's arrival made Granny's death imminent, but my anxiety went deeper. Staring at the eggshell face made me feel that something of Granny was being passed on to me. Her mysterious past, her fragility.

"She's beautiful," Mommy said. "Look at the craftsmanship. The flowers in her hair are intricate. They don't make dolls like this anymore."

I ought to have been grateful. Yet it was as though she embodied everything I'd never understood about my long-lost heritage and my wayward body. The serenity of her face, her impeccable skin, her distant smile, seemed to be mocking me. I wouldn't be able to sleep with that face looking out at me. I had a sudden urge to smash the glass case and pull her kimono apart, layer by layer, living out the fantasy I'd had as a child. Was her head delicate and hollow? Would it break if I squeezed too hard? Or was it dense ceramic that could only be cracked by smashing to the ground?

None of us knew the story behind the doll any more than we knew the story behind Granny. If the doll was just a meaningless gift from some man who'd admired her, why had she hung on to it for seventy years?

It was unsettling to think that if she'd chosen that other life, I would have never been born. In my place, she would have a different granddaughter, who spoke Japanese, had a perfectly straight spine and was brimming with filial piety.

But maybe I was just being silly. The doll didn't hold the key to understanding my origins any more than the Maltese Falcon.

Daddy had clammed up. Whenever I raised questions about Granny and her mother now, he acted as though he'd never confided in me at all.

"Shouldn't you be writing a lecture or something?" he said, as I followed him around the house.

Evidently, I was going to have to take matters into my own hands.

How does Sam Spade do his detective work? Interrogation is one tactic, but he also uses more subtle manoeuvres, which often yield better results. Sometimes he doesn't do anything more than bring the key parties together in the same room and then he just sits back and observes. Harsh words escalate to threats. Lie counters lie and guns get tossed in the air. But throughout it all, even as Spade gets pulled into the violence, he never for a moment stops observing how people reveal themselves as they cover up their lapses, tucking away the information for future use.

So what I wanted to do was create a situation in which Daddy would be compelled to go off on one of his rampages. Now that Granny was barely conscious, I couldn't depend on her to set him off. I racked my brain for something that would get him riled up.

Aunt Tetsuko, Kaz's sister. She knew all the family secrets.

She was perfect. I hadn't seen her all summer – just the excuse to set up a dinner. But when I called and invited her to meet us at her favourite restaurant in Chinatown, her voice sounded shaky. Her hips were bothering her and she no longer liked to leave the house. So I told her we would get takeout and bring it over, since my father missed seeing her.

"Really?" Girlish excitement flooded her voice.

When I told my parents that we were going to see her tomorrow evening, Mommy looked perplexed and Daddy's face clouded.

"Don't you think I've got enough to deal with?" he said.

Aunt Tetsuko lived in an apartment on the first floor of a big old house on Dovercourt. I had fond memories of going for dinners at that house, where she used to make interesting dishes like osso bucco, and the walls were covered in paintings of fruit bowls and nude women, which she'd done years ago, when she was a high-school art teacher. Jazz always played in the background.

It was strange to think of this jolly white-haired lady as Kaz's little sister. I wondered if he was the one who got her interested in art and music.

But she didn't appear too jolly these days. She'd put on weight and wasn't wearing any lipstick. Gazing longingly at the bottle of wine under my arm – just the thing to get her talking – she shook her head. The doctor had told her she had to stop drinking.

113

What had become of her racy tongue, her raucous laughter? It didn't seem natural to see Aunt Tetsuko so painfully sober, and I was reminded of how Hammett had given up drinking in the final years of his life. His doctor had told him he had to go on the wagon or else prepare to die. A shy man, who needed alcohol to be around people at all, Hammett's prognosis spelled the death of his social life. I recalled seeing a photo of him the year before he died; he was an emaciated, white-haired man with slouched shoulders, his expression so vacant it was as if he'd forgotten he was even there.

Aunt Tetsuko had the same empty look, as she hobbled in carrying a tray of plates. The TV was on closed caption in the background, and she kept staring at it longingly. We must have been keeping her from her favourite show.

"Aunt Tetsuko, aren't you going to ask about how my mother is doing?" Daddy said.

"Oh." She rubbed her eyes, like she'd forgotten about Granny's condition completely. "How's your mother?"

"Not so well. She's weak from the surgery. And her other leg's gone bad, too."

"That's too bad. She was always the pretty one. The jewel of the family."

"I guess that's why Kaz was drawn to her." Daddy reached into his pocket for his digital recorder, and ever so discreetly, turned it on. "Could you talk a bit about how Mom and Kaz met?"

I smiled. My plan was working. Daddy couldn't resist talking about the past.

But a gloomy look came over Aunt Tetsuko's face. She hunched down in her chair, burping slightly. "Do I have to? Every time you come over here, Jack, it's 'Talk about this, talk about that.' What if I just want to sit quiet?"

"Oh, come on." The pleading tone of a little boy crept into his voice. "Now that Mom's lost her marbles, who am I going to ask?"

Mommy and I opened the paper bags and set the steaming cartons on the dining room table. We began serving the food, but Daddy wouldn't let the conversation drop.

"I remember the night when we arrived in Toronto by train," he said. "Mom hadn't yet found the house on St. Clarens, so we went to a motel with a neon sign. I woke up on this big armchair – it was covered in green plaid – and I woke up itchy all over. The chair was infested with fleas. I woke up covered in welts. I looked over at the bed and the covers were rumpled, but Mom wasn't there. Kaz had taken her out somewhere. To a bar or out dancing."

Aunt Tetsuko stared out the window, her face expressionless. "All I can say is they were too young to be parents."

Daddy bit into a spring roll. "Oh, come on, it was more than that."

"Jack, what do you want me to say?"

"Kaz always said that you understood him in a way Mom never could," Daddy continued. "You would come over and the two of you would be drinking in the basement, and I could hear your voices from upstairs. What did you talk about?"

"I don't know. It was a long time ago."

"I remember the night Kaz died, you came over that afternoon. Was he asking you for more pills?"

Aunt Tetsuko rubbed her temples. "We all took pills back then. The doctors gave them out like candy. After the war, it was the only way I could sleep."

"Did Kaz have trouble sleeping, too?" I asked.

"I don't know." She rubbed her eyes again. "Kaz needed someone to talk to, because Masako wasn't the most understanding woman. A man would have better luck talking to a vase."

"No one understood Kaz," I said. "Except you."

She smiled weakly. "He was meant to be a musician or artist or something. . . . "

"So why didn't you help him?" Daddy stared at Aunt Tetsuko across the table, but she just kept playing with her soggy spring roll, refusing to meet his gaze.

We listened to the sound of a siren becoming increasingly distant.

"What do you want me to say?" Aunt Tetsuko finally said. "It was Masako's fault as much as mine. She drove him crazy with her ridiculous expectations. He should have left her. I'm sure the thought crossed his mind."

I thought about what it would be like being married to Granny and for the first time, I felt sorry for Kaz.

But Daddy's eyes were shining. "You think he should have left us?"

"I'm sorry, but Kaz just wasn't a family man."

Daddy nodded, but the disbelief in his eyes lingered, as if he were still a stunned child. Hammett had left his wife when their daughters were young. A few years back, I'd read a biography written by his youngest daughter, Jo Hammett, and it touched me how she'd written about her father's departure. At first Hammett moved to separate quarters because of his tuberculosis, but after the illness passed, he never moved back. He wanted his own place where he could drink and play poker and entertain women and write in solitude. Although Jo Hammett gives a remarkably measured account of her eccentric dad, the hurt voice of a little girl comes through as she describes her heartbroken mother.

But Hammett wasn't a family man. And neither was Kaz.

"I know I should have done something to help him," Aunt Tetsuko said. "But what could I do? I was just a student, trying to go back to university after the war. I thought it was just his drinking, that if he stopped, things would get better. . . . "

Daddy shook his head.

She clasped her stomach and ran to the bathroom. Through the door, we heard a waterfall of vomit. It was time for us to go.

chapter seven

When he was born I knew that motherhood was invented by someone who had to have a word for it because the ones that had the children didn't care whether there was a word for it or not.

—William Faulkner, *As I Lay Dying*

"Poplar or cherry?" Daddy said. He slid a brochure across the table.

I stared at the caskets, so solid and heavy, and something about the ruffled satin lining in Pepto-Bismol pink made me giggle. Is that the wall Granny would want to stare at for all eternity?

Daddy had spent the past three days meeting with funeral home directors, comparison shopping, planning ahead for the inevitable. At least it gave him something to do.

"It's big business." He flipped open his laptop to show me a website.

What balls these people had. Who charges $39.95 to light a memorial candle? The website was full of ways to activate your PayPal account, buy services, and even avoid going to the funeral altogether, while appeasing your guilt.

Daddy smiled grudgingly. "Absolutely recession-proof."

"You should have gone into the funeral business."

"Oh, yeah. Can you see me with old ladies crying on my shoulder?"

We continued joking, but something about the whole thing really got to me. Spending all this money and the person being honoured wasn't even around to enjoy it.

"I'd rather just go the way of Addie Bundren," I said.

Daddy looked at me blankly.

I explained that Addie Bundren is the cranky old matriarch at the centre of Faulkner's *As I Lay Dying*. The novel begins on the eve of her death, as her son, Cash, is making her casket, sawing and sanding boards. All her kids – Cash, Darl, Jewel, Dewey Dell and Vardaman – are crowded around her bedside watching her die, just like we were all hovering around Granny. After her death, they pack her into the casket and load the whole thing into a horse-drawn buggy to make an epic journey across the land to Jefferson, Mississippi, where Addie wishes to be buried with her own people, rather than by her husband's side.

"A homemade casket," Daddy said, shaking his head.

"You should read it."

"Maybe I will."

As the novel unfolds, it becomes clear that much more is at stake than just an eccentric lady's dying wish. Addie Bundren wants to be alone. Alone in death. To put the final nail in the coffin of a life lived in solitude and despair.

An image of Granny being carted away by horse and buggy popped into my head. She was no less a strange, impenetrable woman.

A few days later, I was revising the syllabus for my Modern American Literature course (just in case I needed it for next year). Last year I'd deluded myself that undergrads could handle *Absalom! Absalom!* What had I been thinking? Even Faulkner scholars are baffled by what he was up to in telling the legendary story of Thomas Sutpen, in flashbacks by multiple narrators whose accounts fail to match up. The reader is left guessing about who Thomas Sutpen really was.

My course evaluations reflected just how much the students loved the novel (I'd finally forced myself to read through the pile). "What was Faulkner on when he wrote that crap?" wrote one kid. "Half the time I didn't even know who's speaking – everything blended together like a bizarre dream."

Since I would have to teach a Faulkner novel (what's an Am Lit class without Faulkner?), I figured *As I Lay Dying* was a better bet. Although the novel is told from fifteen different perspectives, at least it's always clear who's speaking; each chapter is titled with the name of the speaker. And the plot is simple, deceptively simple. At first glance, you wonder why Faulkner is spilling so much ink over an old lady's death.

But Addie Bundren gradually draws you in. She has shameful secrets at the core of her being. As soon as she dies, the neighbours are all gossiping about how quickly the Bundrens pack her up and cart her off.

I wondered if Granny's neighbours were talking about Daddy. They must have seen him packing boxes at her house.

Despite Daddy's show of wanting to get her death over with, however, I could tell that deep down he was astonished it was happening at all. I could see it in his childlike air, his petulant gaze, the way he stomped around the house. In a way, he reminded me of Vardaman, Addie's youngest son. After her death, Vardaman bursts into the barn; the warm, rank smells envelop him and mix with the smell of his own vomit and tears and everything seems very close and suffocating. The little boy is so overwhelmed that he wants to lash out at something, anything, "You kilt my maw!" burning at the back of his throat.

Yet racing through the dust and striking the horses can't make it better, can't bring his mother back.

Time was running out – and what had I decided?

My long walks around the city grew more aimless and desperate each day. The August humidity was baking my skin. But I didn't care. I just wanted to keep walking, an endless concrete river.

Anything to keep my mind off my dismal prospects.

One day I found myself across the street from my old high school at Yonge and Eglinton. What had once been a dingy mall had been renovated into a gleaming shopping complex, with a hulking Silver City movie theatre and Chapters Indigo bookstore out front. Most of my old haunts had been swept away, but at least Timothy's Coffee was still there. I ordered an Irish Cream and splashed in plenty of milk and sugar, wanting to recapture that taste of so many years ago, that taste of the world being sweet and creamy and full of possibilities.

North Toronto Collegiate looked shabbier than I remembered. I'd read in the paper that the school was slated to be rebuilt as part of an innovative mixed-use development, featuring a massive condo on top. The whole thing made me sad. As I walked down the alley alongside the parking lot, where all the cool kids used to hang out smoking, skipping class, I could almost see their faces, the bright knit toques and dreadlocked hair and loose Guatemalan clothing that flapped in the wind as they kicked around a hacky sack.

Not that I'd ever been part of that crowd. I'd be kidding myself to think I was ever immersed in the thick of their smoke and drunken laughter.

No, I was always watching from the corner of my eye as I whizzed straight ahead, clasping my clarinet case, heading down to a carrel in the basement library. Why was I so scared to loosen up and have fun? But I was shy and awkward and militantly perfectionist about everything from my A-double-pluses to the origami-sharp collars of my shirts, even though, by that point, I had begun to experiment by cultivating friendships with girls who went to other schools or hardly even went to school anymore. Girls who wore leather jackets and had fake ID and drug-dealer boyfriends. Girls who had abusive fathers and nutcase mothers and used to cut themselves just for fun. For some reason, I gravitated to these sweet screw-ups and we bonded instantly, without explanation, catching a scent of each other's drugstore perfume mixed with sweat.

It must have been the smell of each other's desperation. My old friend, Natalie, had been fascinated by the scar across my torso. "That is the coolest thing ever," she said.

I peered through the chalk-streaked windows of the school into the basement classrooms, where my physics and chemistry classes used to be taught. It was like glimpsing my past and seeing my future superimposed on the same frightening image of the lecture podium, floating high above the rows of desks, the air chalky and hot, all eyes on the instructor. I recalled the running jokes about Mr. Carlisle's fat ass and Miss Jamison's green eye shadow, and when one of the guys at the back started the ball rolling – usually Dan Schmidt, with his baseball cap backwards – the class would laugh and enjoy the feeling of ascending a roller coaster, sure to peak with the teacher shouting and turning red.

It left me nauseous thinking about how callous those kids had been. That was me now, the one they were laughing at. Twittering about, mocking on Facebook. I couldn't bear the thought of going back.

"What happened to Granny's mother?" I asked.

"What do you mean, what happened to her?" Daddy continued clipping the hedges in front of our house.

"I remember Aunt Tetsuko saying she wasn't around much when Granny was young."

Daddy looked up and put down the clippers.

She'd been on my mind a lot lately. Every time I passed a dry-cleaning shop and caught a glimpse of a glum woman behind the counter, I'd think of my great-grandmother, the last-minute picture bride. Ayako had been her name. I'd never met her, but Mommy and Aunt Tetsuko used to gossip about her when I was a kid. I remembered Aunt Tetsuko saying, with a knowing raise of her eyebrows, that Ayako would disappear for long periods to get away from the old guy.

"Ayako went away on long trips to Japan," Daddy said. "I guess she missed her family."

"How could she afford to travel back?"

Daddy shrugged. "I expect that by that time the dry-cleaning shop was doing all right. She was a good businesswoman. Very shrewd with money."

I thought back to the photo of Ayako and Granny's father that used to hang in Granny's old house. Her drooping profile, her white dress covered in ruffles. There was a resoluteness to her face – clear, glowing skin and a good, square jaw. She looked like a woman who knew what she wanted. Clutched in her arms was a newborn infant (Granny), and it pained me to notice how puffy Ayako's hands were, swollen from the chemicals used to dry-clean clothes. There was something about the way her shoulders turned away from her grey-haired husband, the baby leaden in her arms, that made me suspect this wasn't the life she'd bargained for. Not by a long shot.

"Ayako was like Addie Bundren," I said.

Daddy nodded. "A lot of women back in the old days were."

I was thinking in particular of the chapter titled "Addie." Here, we get the thoughts and feelings of the dead woman, speaking from beyond the grave, reflecting on her own life. Out come all the things she could never say when she was alive. Addie's marriage to Anse Bundren wasn't driven by anything more than her own desperation and limited opportunities. She hated being a schoolteacher, left to deal with other people's snot-nosed kids, and who can blame her? Anse offered her a way out: a good house, a good farm.

As soon as the slew of babies arrives, however, a new kind of misery sets in. The comforts of domestic life – love, family, home – mean nothing to her. She craves being a girl again, alone and carefree. By claiming to save her, Anse has duped her into a life she despises, where her body feels violated and overworked all the time, turned into one big void.

Had Ayako felt just as trapped? Just as desperate to escape?

Grant was twenty minutes late. I was sitting on the patio of a bar in Yorkville drinking my second gin and tonic all too quickly, a rubber band tightening around my temples.

"Message Received," my phone said in its sing-songy voice.

It was Grant texting me with some lame excuse about how he couldn't make it. His sister had decided to throw their father a surprise birthday party – or so he said. This was the third time he'd cancelled on me. I suspected his girlfriend had cut her vacation in Europe short, in order to keep tabs on him.

The rippling laugh of a woman with impeccable fake nails at the table next to me stabbed into my brain. I quickly settled the bill and left.

The rosy faces of couples, holding hands and licking gelatos, were equally abhorrent. For a moment, I thought that by walking close to them, brushing up against their pink glow of happiness, some of it might rub off on me. But all I got were dirty looks and someone trampled my foot.

My head buzzing from the gin, I found myself wandering down Yonge, jostling against the ladies in shiny heels and pencil-thin skirts, dodging the homeless people who jumped out at me with jack-o-lantern grins. My eyes started watering from the gritty haze. I turned west on Queen, speed-walking. My feet ached, but I kept walking toward nothing in particular, one block bleeding into the next, each block a bit more gritty and colourful.

My thoughts drifted to Granny and how lonely it must have been for her to grow up without her mother. I couldn't imagine what it would be like to be born into such a loveless marriage and tears brimmed my eyes, I felt so bad for her. And then I started thinking about the Bundren kids and how they must have felt with Addie as their mom. The shortest chapter is five words long: "My mother is a fish."

Jewel is the only kid who manages to win her affection at all, and Faulkner slowly reveals the reason. Jewel doesn't look like the others and they hold him at a distance because they know in their gut he isn't one of them. He's Addie's love child – the offspring of her affair with the preacher.

He marks the cleft in the Bundren family, a cleft that runs deep.

Tears streamed down my cheeks and I felt like a perfect idiot with people on the street staring at me, but what did I care? What did it matter if I looked like hell? It wasn't as if I were meeting Grant, and it felt good to just let it all out. The glorious anonymity of the crowd enveloped me. At least I didn't have to worry about running into students or colleagues or the Dean of Arts – I was free to be just some crazy girl having a meltdown on the street.

I wiped my eyes on my sleeve and wandered into one of the more avant-garde galleries on Ossington. The photo exhibit was of Asian sex workers plying their trade in back alleys and government offices, straddling and swishing their hair against the wooden faces of Communist Party officials.

Josh would have found this interesting and my eyes misted up again, as I began imagining the conversation we'd be having if he were here now.

"Well, well, the Party's not over," he'd say. "Check out these cute little comrades."

I stumbled outside, where I sat on the curb for a good while and everything looked grimy and grey. A woman with beautiful tattoos was nice enough to give me a cigarette.

I inhaled deeply, trying to soak up every last breath of urban culture.

When I got home, the house was empty. Daddy was running a fun fly at his model airplane club and Mommy was out of town visiting her sister.

Now was the perfect time to listen to the rest of the recording of Granny. The realization hit me with a wave of sweat.

The digital recorder was folded in a handkerchief and tucked away in the top drawer of Daddy's desk. Guilt fluttered over me, but my thirst to know was simply too great.

I pressed the play button.

Granny's voice was shrill as a little girl's. "Some men came – they were FBI and I was very upset because I didn't know why they were taking away my father. I knew he hadn't done anything against the law."

She was talking about the Japanese-American internment. I'd never heard her talk about any of this before.

"Where was your father taken?" Daddy asked.

"Missoula. Missoula, Montana."

"Didn't you go with him?"

"No. Me, my mother and brother were sent to another camp in Minidoka, Idaho. Later my father came to join us."

"How long were you there?"

"I was there until Kaz came to get me and we got married in the camp. That was in 1943."

"But Kaz was Canadian," Daddy said. "At the war's outbreak, he wouldn't have been allowed to drive down the coast. He had to stay in Kaslo, where his father was running the camp hospital."

A long pause.

"Mom, what was Kaz up to?"

"I told him to go back," Granny said softly. "I told him we could get married after the war. But he was so insistent that we do it now."

"Did he sneak into your camp?"

Another long pause.

"He came to Minidoka and registered as my brother," Granny finally said. "The place was so disorganized – lots of stuff like that happened. The guards didn't care. No one checked paperwork. So Kaz showed up one day, and he was billeted to our room in the barrack. My family was horrified, but what could they do? Everyone was talking. They knew I only had one brother."

"Is that why your parents agreed to let you marry him? Because of the gossip?"

Silence. Presumably, a nod.

So this was how my grandparents' courtship had culminated. She hadn't been in love with him at all. Granny had been a woman in captivity – double captivity, in fact. First, she was interned in the middle of nowhere, and then her life was doubly constrained by her violation or seduction, however you wanted to think about it, and in such a public, humiliating way.

And to top it all off, she'd been forced to marry her seducer in a last-ditch effort at saving face.

"At least after we were married, I got to move to Canada," Granny said. "We went to Kaslo and lived in Dr. Shimo's house. It wasn't so bad. It was a nice house on the edge of the camp there. I could come and go as I pleased."

She continued talking with such forced brightness.

But as I listened, something heavier edged into her voice, and my thoughts drifted to Addie Bundren. I wondered what my grandmother would say, given the opportunity to speak beyond the grave and express her real motivations for going to the altar with Kaz.

For how long had I been listening?

Daddy had jumped ahead to their life after the war.

"I remember going to Portland when I was young, Mom. It was before Wendy was born; it was just the two of us. We were living in Verdun. You pulled me out of school one morning and we took a long train trip."

"Oh, you remember Portland?" Granny's voice wavered, like a dying record.

"Of course, Mom," Daddy said. "How long did we stay with your parents? It must have been over a month."

Granny said nothing.

"Why did you pull me out of school?" Daddy asked. "Why did we go, just the two of us?"

"Oh, didn't Kaz go with us?"

"No, Mom." Daddy's tone went icy.

"Well, maybe he had to work. He'd started that business manufacturing ladies' clothes. . . . "

"No, Mom. Don't you remember? That business went bankrupt."

"I don't remember that."

"Yes, Mom. Kaz wasn't doing much of anything."

"Well, it was hard on him. He thought that being Dr. Shimo's son would open doors for him, but after the war, no one cared about any of that. In Verdun and Toronto no one had even heard of the Shimotakaharas."

"Why do you always make excuses for him? He made his own bed."

They lapsed into silence.

"A Jap's a Jap," Daddy said. "Do you remember that wartime saying, Mom? We used to hear it on the radio all the time."

"Maybe I thought it would be nice for us to go on a trip ourselves. Didn't I tell you we would see antelope and bison on the train?"

"Yeah, but we didn't see any. . . . Mom, were you thinking of leaving Kaz? Were you thinking we might stay in Portland, just the two of us?"

The plaintive sound of Daddy's voice filled my eyes with tears, and guilt washed over me.

Granny's voice turned cold. "I'm tired. I don't want to talk anymore."

A car pulled into the driveway. I switched the recorder off and tucked it away.

Under some newspapers on the counter, I found a dog-eared copy of *As I Lay Dying*.

"How much have you read?" I asked.

Daddy looked up. "More than half. Is Yoknatoffee even a real place?"

"Yoknapatawpha County." When I'd first started reading Faulkner, I'd hardly been able to pronounce it either, and I still made a point of never saying it when I was teaching. There's nothing so embarrassing as getting tongue-tied in the midst of your own lecture.

"So is it real?"

"Depends on how you look at it." Yoknapatawpha, I explained, is the southern county Faulkner invented, loosely based on Oxford, Mississippi, where he was born and spent most of his life. It's a place of economic decline and decayed gentility; the novels he sets there take place in the decades after the Civil War, when the old southern families and good ole boys, like the Bundrens, are being turned into white trash. Meanwhile, a new kind of southerner, who's brash and business-minded, is on the rise.

But for all its failings, this place is home for Faulkner. The glory, the tragedy and all the injustices of the Old South intermingle in his writing, filling him with love and hate in equal measure. Maybe that's how we all feel about home.

"Why didn't Faulkner just set his novels in Oxford, Mississippi?" Daddy asked.

"Because he wanted to make clear that it's *not* a real place. He's created a fictional landscape where he can explore a fantasy of how his ancestors lived."

"Faulkner yearned to recreate his roots."

I nodded, my smile mirroring Daddy's, and I could guess what he was thinking. Kaz and Granny were like characters out of a Faulkner novel. And like Faulkner, we were obsessed by our past.

"At first I didn't like her," Daddy said, "but now I feel sorry for Addie Bundren. Her sons are at each other's throats, her daughter's knocked up and her husband's more interested in getting false teeth than mourning her death."

I laughed. "Yeah, the family's falling apart. Have you got to the part where they're crossing the ford?"

"That scene's pretty good."

Packed into their wagon with the coffin in tow, the Bundrens are trying to cross the ford, but a log gets in the way and the wagon tips over. Cash crashes into the water, injuring his leg, and all the mules are killed.

"I feel bad for Addie," Daddy said. "No doubt, she wasn't the nicest mother, but look what she had to deal with." A shadow crossed his face.

The past few nights, I hadn't been sleeping well. I'd close my eyes and all I could see were the mint-green walls of my old apartment in Antigonish, blurring into the puke-green walls of Granny's hospital room. I didn't want to stay, I didn't want to go. My jaw ached like I'd been grinding on sandpaper all night.

The microwave clock said 4:47, as I felt my way through the inky darkness and touched a cupboard.

"Since you're up, there's something I want to show you."

I was so startled I nearly dropped my mug.

I followed Daddy into the family room, where his laptop lay open on the sofa, along with a crumpled bag of chips. His skin looked grey, like he hadn't slept in a while either.

"Look what I found." He pointed at the screen. "I googled Minidoka, the camp where Granny was interned, and found some pictures online. I'm pretty sure it's her."

The black-and-white photo depicted a group of young Japanese women in front of a dreary wooden building. They were raking mud, their heads bent, their flowered cotton dresses blowing in the wind. The whole thing looked so choreographed, so ridiculously stage-managed – probably by some government photographer – that they might have been the chorus in a musical. Stepping forward to do a silly dance.

"That's Granny," Daddy said. "The girl one in from the right."

It was strange to see this slip of a woman, barely older than a teenager, and recognize in her profile my grandmother's face. Weird thoughts rushed through my mind. I found myself looking at the careful styling of her hair and wondering how, while living in an internment camp, she could manage to keep it freshly curled and glossy – while I, from the comfort of home, could barely make the effort to blow-dry. But even imprisoned and made to rake mud, my grandmother would not let herself go. Her instinct for self-preservation should have made me happy, but it made me feel like shit.

And while the other girls are working, she appears to be only pretending to work – something about the whimsical tilt of her head. She's caught in a moment of fantasy or denial, her mind a thousand miles away.

All the frailties of her personality seemed to be encapsulated in that image.

I wondered if by that point Kaz had arrived at the camp. Was that the source of the secretive smile playing on her lips? What had she felt for him back then?

What my father had recorded were the words of an old woman looking back on the past through the distortion of memory, disappointment, shame. But at the time, what had she really felt?

I'd wondered if Kaz had practically raped her, but now as I examined her bright eyes and ballerina posture, another set of imaginative possibilities opened up. I imagined her pulse racing and a bright light filling her head, just knowing that a man was obsessed with her – so obsessed, he'd followed her to this godforsaken place.

Perhaps she'd been a carefree girl who knows she's pretty and enjoys just revelling in her own independence, like the young Addie Bundren.

But at some point, the light faded from her eyes. It must have dawned on her – perhaps all of a sudden, one day after the war – that she was married to a drunk, a fool, a madman. By then, it was all too late.

Was it abnormal for me to be taking this prurient interest in my grandmother's love life? Was it weird that I wanted to slip into her sensuous skin?

If so, I blame it wholly on my longstanding history of reading novels.

I'd spent too many days of my childhood with *Jane Eyre*, poring over the pages where we learn the secret that Rochester's first wife, a madwoman, has been held captive in his attic for years. Maybe a sex slave. Why else would he keep her there?

And despite my three degrees, sense was the last thing on my mind whenever I reread *Sense and Sensibility*. I sympathized all too well with Marianne Dashwood's wayward heart – the cause of her undoing. The masochistic joy and humiliation of throwing herself at a man who isn't even available. I had her number down pat.

Sexual secrets and their delicious exposure. This is what's at the core of the novel form.

So I couldn't help it that after all these years of novel reading, I'd come to envision myself as the heroine of a novel – rooting out perversion in my own family, at once shocked and titillated, my own body wrestling with desire, as I fantasized at some level about doing the unthinkable myself. Becoming a fallen woman. For they're the most interesting characters of all – these ladies who cross over to the other side of the social tapestry, where darkness, mania, sexual impropriety and the spectre of rape loom large.

Granny emerged in my mind as having something of this "fallen" quality. That was why I found her so compelling. She marked the other, darker side of myself.

Mommy got back from her trip, and not a moment too soon. There were certain things I needed to get straight.

"Hey, Mommy," I said. "Did Tetsuko ever tell you anything about why Granny's mother kept making trips to Japan?"

Mommy looked astonished. "I didn't know you were eavesdropping. I assumed you were too little to understand what we were talking about."

"Well, I'm not too little now."

She looked at me conspiratorially and lowered her voice. "Now you must swear you'll keep this in the strictest confidence. This isn't the sort of thing you can be blurting out at a family dinner."

I nodded meekly.

"Don't say I didn't warn you," she said. "This is top secret."

I nodded again.

"Ayako had a lover in Japan."

"What?"

Mommy smiled, doling out the information slowly. "Tetsuko told me he was a businessman who divided his time between Portland and Toyama. Ayako met him on the ship when she was going back to visit her family. They fell in love while crossing the ocean. Year after year, he paid for her ticket back."

He must have been her Peter Walsh. . . . Images and emotions battered my brain. But I couldn't imagine what the affair must have done to her family. No wonder Granny's family reminded me of the Bundrens. I'd detected in Ayako's resolute expression a woman used to getting her way. Her marriage might have been rotten to the core, but she'd taken her pleasures where she could. She'd had her fun with the preacher.

Mommy pursed her lips, as if she couldn't decide whether to reveal more. "When Granny's father found out about the affair, he went stark raving mad."

She said that Daddy remembered taking a trip to Portland as a little boy and visiting his grandfather in a big white house that turned out to be an asylum. Granny had to have her father committed, after he'd attacked her.

"What a family," I said, my mind racing.

Mommy's eyes misted over. "I can't believe Ayako left Granny with that nutcase when she was away in Japan. You don't do that to your little girl."

Tears were running down my cheeks, too. Finding out the truth didn't feel so good. Maybe I was better off spending my life barricaded in a library.

"Ironically, having a crazy father was good preparation for her life with Kaz," Mommy added.

I opened the album and turned to the picture of Granny after she'd given birth. Her startled expression and the childlike fright in her eyes drew me in. She was a girl used to being on guard. Even as she cradled the newborn to her chest, she looked distant. Her thoughts were elsewhere, yearning for some plan of escape.

chapter eight

"Oh Jake," Brett said, "we could have had such a damned good time together."

"Yes," I said. "Isn't it pretty to think so?"

-Ernest Hemingway, *The Sun Also Rises*

I was lying on my bedroom floor, my head next to the vent. The stream of chilled air washed over me, until I might have been in a morgue.

Laundry was piled up in the corner. The campus bookstore kept emailing me asking why I hadn't placed the orders for my courses. There were *countless* things on my to-do list. But it was easier to just keep lying here, pretending I was dead.

Shouldn't I have left this state behind as a teenager?

I went down to the living room, where Daddy was stretched out on the couch, his limbs sprawled everywhere. It was as if he'd done it just to spite me. Just to prevent me from flinging myself down.

"You must be looking forward to getting back to your real life," he said.

"What are you talking about? Haven't you been listening to anything I've been saying all summer?"

"But you've invested so much time in your academic career. I'm sure that if you stick it out, things will get better."

"I don't know, Daddy. I just don't know."

His smile faded, and it was satisfying to see his unease. I wanted him to worry that I was teetering on the edge of madness, like all my sorry-ass ancestors.

He peered over to see what I was reading. It irked me that just because we'd read a few books together, he felt entitled to act like we were comrades. I told him that I just didn't have time to tell him about it. If he was so curious, he should pick up his own copy of *The Sun Also Rises*.

Sounding more than a little hurt, he said he might. My stomach flip-flopped.

Soon it would be back to all the intellectual bullshit and posturing and at the end of the day, I'd be coming home to an empty apartment. Reading alone.

Josh called that night. Actually, he'd been calling rather a lot lately. He would be working late at the office and around eleven he'd get chatty.

"So what did you read today?" Night after night, he asked the same question. He seemed to think that all I did was lounge around reading all day, his voice sharp with envy. But in a way, I was glad that he thought I was happy.

I told him that I was reading *The Sun Also Rises*. I was thinking about teaching it in the fall.

"I remember when you first read that novel," he said. "It was the summer you followed me to Japan."

"Followed you?" Blood rushed to my cheeks. "If I remember correctly, you begged me to come."

"Oh, right." His voice froze over. He didn't want to go into it. Our miserable summer in Japan.

Everything had fallen apart the summer after Josh graduated. I still had another two years left at McGill, but he found himself at loose ends. He'd been planning to apply to law school in Toronto and New York, and we were going to continue our relationship long-distance. But at the last minute, Josh got another idea. One of his profs had told him about a scholarship program that allowed foreigners to do a Masters at Osaka University and without telling me, he'd applied to the history department.

He wasn't ready to become a straitlaced lawyer, he said. He needed to have big adventures first. He needed to find himself. These cheesy words actually crossed his lips.

So he was moving to Osaka for the next three years and I was welcome to visit anytime. Anytime I felt like flying to the other side of the world.

I remembered how enraged I'd been at how easily, how calmly, he could leave me. My first thought had been that this was his covert way of breaking up – he was just too cowardly to come out and say it. Yet when I confronted him, he insisted he wanted to be with me. Down the road, he saw us having a brood of cute "Jewpinese" kids. (Josh marvelled at how many Jewish guys hooked up with Japanese girls). It was just that right now he needed to be on his own.

What was it that he found so damn enticing about Japan anyway? He'd gone there twice to teach English already, the year after he finished high school and the summer between second and third year. Josh had shown me photos of his binges at foreigner bars: he'd be dressed in outlandish fluorescent T-shirts and ripped jeans, a *yukata* draped over top like a smoking jacket, while making a peace sign, cute Japanese girls and sunburnt Australians crowded in the background. Who did he think he was? John Lennon? I felt embarrassed just looking at the pictures.

"What is it you love about Japan?"

"I don't know," he said. "I just feel most like myself when I'm there."

Now that I thought about it, Josh's lust for the ex-pat life reminded me of Jake Barnes in *The Sun Also Rises*. Jake is American – a true Midwesterner – yet Paris is where he feels most at home. When a prostitute asks him if his name is Flemish, he retorts that he's nothing other than American. It's at these moments of feeling most estranged from his true self that, ironically, he feels most himself. For all his searching and drunken misery and turmoil in love, Jake is oddly content being lost in Paris.

Josh had a similar perverse love of Japan.

After he'd left for Japan, I was a wreck. A week went by. Two weeks. I wondered if he was thinking about me at all.

And then he called. He'd been out drinking all night and his voice sounded raspy, but it didn't matter because he said we had to be together. It was cherry blossom season in Osaka and he was haunted by strange dreams about the two of us walking under the falling petals. He wanted me to come immediately. I pictured pink streamers falling down on our heads after a birthday party. He was desperately lonely and my eyes filled with tears of happiness.

I called my dad and said I wanted to teach English in Japan for the summer. He bought me a plane ticket the very next day.

But something was off between us from the moment I stepped off the plane. Josh appeared a bit pudgier than I remembered, and his eyes were bloodshot. The apartment he'd rented turned out to be in a shady part of the city, inhabited by yakuza and prostitutes. A stream of sweaty Japanese and Australian businessmen passed through our cramped, dark hallway, and I never felt comfortable stepping out by myself. But Josh was busy attending classes, so what choice did I have?

Alone, I wandered through the crowded streets, dizzy from the flashing lights and whirring Pachinko parlours, staring at the pale, moon-shaped faces drifting by. The women were wearing so much make-up that their faces appeared made of plaster of Paris, silty and wet in the humidity. Didn't it itch? Their high heels clip-clopped down the pavement, Burberry umbrellas swinging against their hips.

It was unsettling to think that we shared the same blood. If my ancestors hadn't immigrated to Canada, would I be one of them? Would I be one of these beautiful automatons?

"Why don't you make an effort to learn Japanese?" Josh said, looking worried. He'd even lent me his old textbook.

But I was too self-conscious to speak pidgin anything. This meant that at restaurants I was dependent on him to order my plate of sushi, to get another beer. What did I care if waitresses looked at me like a freak?

They were *always* staring at me. When I'd say nothing, the waitress would stand there with her pen poised, biting her lip, leaving pink smears on her front teeth.

Josh to the rescue. Suddenly, he'd be pointing at the menu, his voice flooding the table.

What were they talking about? The girl's voice had an automated quality, like the voice that announced the names of subway stations. Each syllable was perfectly placed. The more I'd watch, the more I was struck by some elusive, unreal quality.

Trills of canned laughter. Although I could only guess at what she was saying, I gathered it had something to do with Josh's mastery of the language. Had this chick never met a white guy capable of stringing together a sentence?

"Are you always so friendly with waitresses?"

"It's a good chance to practice my Japanese."

"Oh, right. Like you need any practice. It must really pump you up, the way girls glom onto you here."

Josh put down his beer a little harder than necessary. "What's up with you? I thought we were having a nice lunch."

Not only were we fighting constantly, our sex life had deteriorated as well. It was hell. Throughout all our turbulent periods in the past, sex had been the glue that held us together. But now, I felt repulsed by the way he looked at me with the same milky, blasé eyes that he cast around the room, checking out the other Japanese girls.

I felt a rise in my chest. "Rice chaser."

I knew I was pressing a button. Late at night Josh had confessed that he worried people saw him as just a guy with yellow fever. A rice chaser. I wasn't familiar with these terms at first, so he'd explained: "Oh, you know, one of those guys who doesn't have enough of a schlong, so he heads to the Orient, where life is easy and the women are cute."

"Rice chaser," I repeated.

His eyes flashed, a mix of hurt and fear. "You didn't even know what that meant before I told you."

"It's funny," Daddy said, flipping through *The Sun Also Rises*. "Even though Jake Barnes is impotent, he still seems manly."

Injured in the First World War, Jake has lost his balls. (Hemingway never makes clear whether he's literally lost his balls, or whether his impotence is more of a psychological condition, but in any case, he can't get it up).

Still, women fall madly in love with Jake, and Daddy was right – he always seems perfectly masculine, in control.

"You really feel his suffering," he continued. "But Jake never seems wimpy. I like the guy."

I liked him, too. I remembered when I'd first read *The Sun Also Rises* that summer in Japan, I'd sympathized all too well with Jake's impotence.

At first, there's something tantalizing about how Jake and Lady Brett Ashley lust after each other, despite the fact they can't consummate their passion. But the sweet torture soon becomes torture, plain and simple. As Jake watches Brett seduce other men under his nose, he comes to despise her – even though he still loves her – and his impotence takes on a larger meaning. The reader is forced to wonder: even if Jake could get it up, would this couple stand a chance?

Brett loves her freedom far too much to settle down with her own true love. The more I'd read, the more my own doubts had grown. Why couldn't

Josh and I get it together? Did we stand a chance?

But that was all so long ago; why was I rehashing it now?

"What do you think of Jake and Brett's relationship?" I asked.

"It's a shame they can't be together," Daddy said. "They're so much in love."

I remembered people saying the same thing about me and Josh. All our breakups and tearful reconciliations left our friends perplexed. I recalled the sensation of walking down the street with him, arm in arm, and it felt so natural, so easy, that we might have been floating on air.

But then there were all the dark times. There were a lot of dark times after I left Japan. Josh was furious that I chose to come home early, but what did he expect? I became ill with a nasty bladder infection and the doctor wouldn't prescribe antibiotics. I felt like knives were cutting through my gut. Yet the doctor insisted it was all in my head.

We didn't speak for months, but then the phone calls started again and all the old hopes were revived. Soon we were sending each other love letters and homemade cards with silly drawings in Magic Marker and we were convinced that we had to be together. I'd come home to an empty apartment, as lonely as Jake Barnes, and then Josh would call and all the longing and torture would start again. My heart fluttered every time he told me how miserable he was in Japan.

Still, it drove me insane, the thought of him dating other women. Those cutesy Japanese girls.

Our bodies ached for each other. We had phone sex – hot, raunchy phone sex – that began with the age-old formula of *Imagine that if I were there beside you, I would be doing this to you now....*

Then we would repeat how much we missed each other and make plans to see each other over the Christmas holidays.

But when we saw each other, things were bad again. Our libidos plummeted, and the old feelings of impotence set in.

"What are you thinking about?" Daddy said. "For the past five minutes, you've been staring into space."

I blinked and returned to my bowl of Cheerios, now soggy.

"Oh, I was just thinking about Josh. I think I really missed the boat on him." Salty tears were filling my eyes.

"That was years ago." Daddy looked alarmed.

"Yeah, well, what do you want me to say?"

"He was never right for you."

"Thanks for reminding me," I said. "You never liked him anyway."

"Oh, Leslie," Daddy said. "I just wanted you to be happy. You were crying all the time."

I continued staring into my cereal.

"Why so glum?"

"My life sucks. I have no idea what I'm doing with myself."

Daddy frowned. "You didn't use to be this way. You used to have gumption."

"What are you talking about? I was a sickly kid who couldn't stand up straight. I spent half my childhood going in and out of hospitals."

"That's not true," he said. "Don't you remember your clarinet recital?"

Daddy was talking about a day so long ago I could hardly believe that girl had been me. I must have been about ten at the time. It was the year everyone in my class was expected to take up a musical instrument. I'd chosen clarinet somewhat arbitrarily, after seeing an older girl, a slender blonde, holding the instrument at our school concert. But Daddy had been excited by my choice because I could be in the marching band down the road, if I were any good; he'd played the trumpet in his high school's marching band back in the day.

Sadly, it soon became clear that my sense of rhythm was about on par with my sense of direction. Whenever I'd practice, my parents would go around the corner for a long coffee. They enrolled me in private lessons and

I got a tiny bit less painful to listen to, but let's just say I was never going to be Benny Goodman.

My music teacher decided to host a concert and Daddy was eager to see me perform. But the Saturday of the concert, fate conspired against me. That afternoon, we drove to the country to cut down our Christmas tree. As we were walking back to the car, I slipped on a patch of ice and fell flat on my face. My nose gushed blood. My lip swelled up. And I had only three hours until I was expected to play.

"We obviously can't go," Mommy said. "You have to lie down."

"I'm fine," I shouted. "I've been practicing all month."

"Try an ice pack," Daddy said.

So for the next two hours, I sat with a bag of frozen peas strapped to my face – intent on getting up in front of that audience.

And I did. I played right through my *fughetta* and only squeaked once. Daddy was sitting at the front of the church beaming.

It felt like a lifetime since I'd seen that look on his face.

"Can we talk about something?" Josh asked.

It was the tone he used whenever he wanted to talk about something heavy. Sweat prickled my armpits and I knew that now I'd never get to sleep. These late-night phone calls were taking a toll on me.

"Okay," I said.

"I've been thinking about what happened between us all those years ago. I want you to know that when things ended, I was left in an emotional wilderness for two years."

I stared out my window at a teenage girl walking her dog, and now the dog was crapping on our lawn.

"As I thought back on things," he continued, "it depressed me that we never had a proper courtship."

Emotional wilderness? Proper courtship?

"This isn't Victorian England." I laughed, but he remained silent. Yes, he was in the mood for a heavy talk indeed.

"Do you remember the bullfight scene in *The Sun Also Rises?*" Josh asked.

"Of course."

Jealousy, rivalry, violence. . . . Everything culminates in the bullfight scene. Jake, Brett and their friends head to Pamplona for bullfighting season to blow off steam, but the violence in the ring only intensifies the rising emotions within the group. Brett's fiancé, Mike Campbell, has arrived on the scene, but this doesn't stop her from taking a slew of new lovers. Robert Cohn is still gloating about their weekend together in San Sebastian, enraging Jake and Mike. And Romero, this hot, young bullfighter, appears to be Brett's latest conquest. Men offer themselves up to her, ready to be slaughtered, and Mike takes a perverse pleasure in allowing Brett her freedom.

What a bloody mess these people make of their lives.

"You always reminded me of Brett Ashley," Josh said.

I swallowed hard, a slight burning in my chest. "You were the one who wanted an open relationship."

"Not true," he said. "You were the one who suggested it."

"Yeah, but only because I thought it was what you wanted. And it struck me as . . . exciting. Avant-garde or something."

Reading about the fluid and experimental sexual antics of Virginia Woolf and the Bloomsbury coterie had left an indelible impression on my imagination. Not that I'd ended up exercising my freedom to the extent that I'd imagined a woman in an open relationship ought to. But I just liked the *idea* of unbridled sexuality – it made me feel more creative. Josh, for all his whining, had probably taken advantage of our flexible arrangement more than I had.

"Well, the whole thing just made me feel like crap," he said.

"I wouldn't do it again either. I guess it was just something I needed to get out of my system."

It depressed me to think about Hemingway's own miserable love life – his four marriages and multiple mistresses. Did he ever have a satisfying relationship with anyone? I recalled reading in one biography that he'd gotten into the habit of rejecting women before they could reject him, all because he'd been heartbroken by his first love. While driving an ambulance in the First World War, he'd suffered shrapnel wounds and been sent to recuperate at a hospital in Milan, where he fell madly in love with a nurse. Apparently, they'd planned to marry – until Hemingway learned of her engagement to an Italian officer. Devastated, he never could allow himself to trust again or become vulnerable.

"Are you still there?" Josh said.

"Can we talk later? I have to go now."

A manic mouse was scaling the walls of my stomach. I wondered if Josh had a girlfriend, or if he was coming out of a bad relationship and that was why he'd become obsessed with the past. As usual, we were very careful not to mention anything about our love lives. It was our unspoken rule: don't ask, don't tell. I wanted to know, but I didn't want to know. I knew our relationship was hopeless, yet I wanted to believe that we might have a second chance.

Whenever I started to think about a literary concept, I had this bad habit of seeing its permutations everywhere in my own life. It was the complete opposite of what I was supposed to do as a scholar of literature – maintain critical distance, be objective about the text. The text was the text. It wasn't supposed to be about me and my messed-up relationships and my even more messed-up ancestors. I knew all this on a rational level, but I couldn't help the way my natural instincts led me to see the story in terms of my personal life.

And now bullfighting was running rampant across my imagination. Everywhere I looked, I saw jealousy and love triangles and sad, broken relationships. On talk shows, in trailers for movies, eavesdropping on conversations on the subway. Flipping through my father's photo album. I found myself staring at the photos for hours, searching the faces of my dead or near-dead relatives for some kernel of insight, but I had no idea what I was hoping to find.

One picture kept catching my attention. It was the one of Kaz and Haruki, with Granny nestled in between. This picture fascinated me because it always seemed to be changing. The first time I saw it I was struck by Kaz's good looks and confidence, but now there appeared something forced about his smile. And there seemed to be something odd about the photo's composition. It made me uncomfortable the way Granny was standing closer to Haruki than Kaz, and Haruki's arm was draped over her shoulder. Even though Kaz was the more handsome of the brothers, Haruki seemed to have a more natural confidence about his face, a gentle, relaxed quality. Kaz, on the other side, looked tense and defiant, puffing out his chest.

But Granny was smiling at Haruki. If she hadn't been holding Kaz's hand, she and Haruki might appear to be a couple.

"Were Granny and Uncle Haruki close?" I asked.

Daddy glanced at the photo and said nothing. His copy of *The Sun Also Rises* lay open on the coffee table.

"Where was this picture taken?" I asked.

"In Verdun," Daddy said. "On Brown Boulevard, where we shared an apartment with Uncle Haruki."

"Why did you move to Toronto?"

"I don't know. That was never all that clear to me."

"How old were you?"

"Three or four maybe. I don't remember much."

"What do you remember?" I was venturing onto shaky ground, but it was a good sign that Daddy hadn't snapped yet.

"Kaz flew into a rage one morning and said we had to leave town. Mom asked him why and he said it was obvious and then he slapped her and I started crying."

Daddy told me he'd once tried to ask Aunt Tetsuko about what happened. She'd also lived with them in Verdun after the war. But upon being confronted, Aunt Tetsuko didn't want to talk about it. She clammed up and didn't return Daddy's calls for a year.

"What do you think happened?" I said.

"Kaz was always so jealous. . . . Haruki was finishing med school, getting ready to set up his practice. Meanwhile, Kaz wasn't doing much of anything."

"But it must have been more than that," I ventured. "Did it have something to do with Granny?"

Daddy slumped down in his chair. "It was weird how Kaz never wanted Haruki around her."

"Granny had come between them?"

"I remember coming home from school one day," Daddy continued. "This was years later. We were living in Toronto, on St. Clarens. I must have been ten by this point. Anyway, I came home from school and Uncle Haruki had arrived. I guess he was visiting. But Kaz didn't want him there. I walked into the front hall and they were going at it."

"Going at it how?"

"Fighting. They were taking swings at each other and their faces were all red and I could smell the sweat and whiskey."

"Where was Granny?"

"Hiding upstairs. Every so often, she'd peek down and cry out."

I pictured my dad as a little boy standing in the hallway, dumbstruck.

"Later that night," he continued, "Kaz started in on Mom. I was hiding in a closet but it didn't block the noise. The breaking dishes. The screaming.

He was taunting Mom, saying she'd married the wrong Shimotakahara."

"She had married the wrong brother," I said. "No question about that."

Granny had always spoken fondly of Haruki. Too fondly. Years ago, at his funeral, I remembered her standing by the wall, looking bewildered, holding a teacup that rattled in its saucer as I approached.

"Haruki was a great man," she said. "A doctor, like his father." Her face rippled, like an empty pond.

At the time, I hadn't thought much of her sadness, but now I wondered. Granny must have been thinking about Kaz's funeral, decades earlier. And now his brother was dead.

The Shimotakahara she should have married.

There had always been a hint of disdain in how she treated Haruki's wife, Kaoru. Once, when Granny had had too much wine at dinner, she'd launched into a story about how intent Kaoru had been on marrying the next Dr. Shimo. Granny had laughed at how shrewd Kaoru had been, but her eyes flashed as she told the story, jealousy written all over her face.

"You know who Kaz reminds me of?" Daddy said. "Mike Campbell."

"You're thinking of the fiesta scene in *The Sun Also Rises*," I said.

Daddy nodded. "Yeah, he was a mean drunk."

"You are all a lost generation," Gertrude Stein once said to Hemingway, and he used this line as his novel's epigraph. A lost generation. Kaz had been lost, too.

It must have been devastating to have his dreams dashed, while his brother prospered and his wife slipped away. Tears stung my eyes and for the first time I felt a weird closeness to my grandfather.

Before going to bed, I decided to check my email. There were a bunch of messages from students requesting advance copies of the syllabuses for my courses. God, the hamster wheel was starting already.

Looking for some distraction, I turned to Facebook. I'd only joined

Facebook a month ago and I still wasn't terribly familiar with how it worked. Josh and I had recently become Facebook friends, but I hadn't had a chance to examine his profile. He was the first friend who interested me enough to want to peruse his photos.

There were pictures of him making silly, endearing faces with a bunch of Japanese guys at some bar, the pyramid of beer bottles about to topple down. Other photos showed him cycling around New York in his electric blue racing gear. There were close-ups of his bikes – racing bikes, mountain bikes, vintage parts. How many did he have anyway? The number seemed to have tripled since we'd broken up.

My eyes skimmed over the photos and settled on the face of a Japanese girl. "Yuki and Josh" read the tag. They were sitting at a kitchen table, eating noodles, smiling at each other, gloriously at ease in each other's presence. She was in several other pictures, too – in some, her hair was cut in a funky bob, in others, she had a ponytail. It appeared they'd travelled all over Japan, and now they were living in New York.

My stomach wobbled, but I couldn't look away.

I zoomed in on her face, examining her bronzed skin and almond eyes. I hated to admit it, but she was attractive, in a very natural way. She wore no makeup, unusual for a Japanese woman, and she smiled broadly, showing her imperfect teeth, as if flaunting how comfortable she was in her own skin. Yuki. The more I looked at her, the more her face appeared eerily familiar.

Didn't Josh use to have a friend named Yuki that summer I'd visited him in Osaka? Where had he met her? She might have been one of his classmates at the university or the girlfriend of a classmate. He'd been surrounded by so many girls.

It was coming back to me now. Yuki had invited us over for lunch one Sunday. She lived with her family in a tall narrow house, the floors covered in tatami mats. I was expecting Japanese food, but she'd cooked this pasta with a savoury eggplant and tomato sauce. The secret, she'd told me, with a wink, was to add a shot of soy sauce, right into the tomato.

Ooh, gross.

But I had to admit that pasta had tasted delicious.

She'd also made a pitcher of freshly squeezed lemonade and its tartness still remained with me. I could see the round glass pitcher sitting on the counter, the translucent yellow liquid filtering the sun.

I wondered if Josh was so well fed every day.

My fingers trembling, I read through the rest of his profile.

Relationship Status: Married.

Married. The word reverberated against the walls of my head.

The past two months of late-night conversations, the flurry of text messages – what had all *that* been about? Suddenly, everything seemed humiliating, so humiliating. What had he been thinking in reaching out to me? Where did he get off – acting so available?

It was a game, of course. I'd hurt him by dumping him all those years ago and now he was evening the score. All along we'd been playing this pathetic, fucked-up game.

I curled up in the corner of my bed, too numb to even cry, recoiling from the glowing screen of my computer. I wished I'd never opened a Facebook account. I didn't want to connect with anyone, least of all the boy who'd broken my heart.

chapter nine

There was one fine thing about this room that had been the scene of so many defeats and triumphs. From the window he could see, far away, just on the horizon, a long, blue, hazy smear – Lake Michigan, the inland sea of his childhood.

-Willa Cather, *The Professor's House*

I wandered around the house, collecting my things. I had books stacked by the fireplace and tucked under cushions on the sofa. I had sandals in the front hall closet, jumbled up with flattened sneakers.

As I gathered my stuff, I peered at the faded pressed flowers my mother had framed all over the house, memorabilia of trips she'd taken with my father. A watercolour her friend had done also hung on the wall, along with a smattering of more impressive oil paintings they'd bought in Yorkville. None of it was my taste, yet I already missed these familiar images.

In a week, I'd be on my own again. In a basement apartment with bare walls, everything smelling of mildew.

"Back to your studies," Daddy said, smiling approvingly. He handed me a couple more books I'd forgotten.

His approach of pretending everything was just fine reminded me of how he'd dealt with my back crisis all those years ago. While Mommy overcompensated with her sympathetic stares, Daddy assumed a stoic stance and made it clear that I should do the same.

"So you're holding up okay?" had been the extent of his sympathy.

But I hadn't been okay, and I still wasn't. I was tired of holding up his illusion that I was just fine.

"You know the life of the mind isn't all it's cracked up to be."

"It's got to be a lot more fun than carrying a tray of dirty dishes."

"I'd make a lot more money waiting tables, and probably be a lot more mentally healthy."

"Oh, cut the crap. You love your job."

"I do *not*. Do you have any idea of the mental illness in academia – even among top professors? One day, you suddenly snap and want to kill yourself. If you want to know what the life of the mind's really like, read Willa Cather's *The Professor's House*."

Daddy rolled his eyes, but I could see he was curious. More than once, he'd asked me what a typical day at the university consisted of, and I'd blown him off. Well, let him read *The Professor's House* and find out.

It dawned on me as I kept aimlessly walking around the house that I felt a weird identification with Professor St. Peter. The novel opens as St. Peter is in the process of packing, getting ready to move to a luxurious new house. Although he should be on cloud nine, having won a prestigious prize that has given him the money to build the new house, he's depressed beyond belief. Yet nothing's really wrong. It's just this overbearing feeling that the best years of his life are behind him, and now that he's at the top of his game, the rewards seem meaningless.

So he digs in his heels. He refuses to leave his old house. His wife moves to the new house, while St. Peter remains holed up in his attic study, supposedly to finish his book. But he isn't writing. All he does is stare out the window at Lake Michigan, triggering memories of the lakeside town where he grew up, propelling him back on a never-ending search for that place called "home."

Maybe I'd stay put in my room, too. I stared out my bedroom window, but all I could see was the endless grey sky.

Sadly, curling up in a ball wasn't an option. A few weeks earlier, I'd mailed off a deposit. Two deposits, actually.

As it became clear that my fate was sealed for another year, I'd decided to bite the bullet and take the basement apartment with Ben. Even if it were an utter dive, at $240 per month, who could complain? And I'd hardly ever be there. Friday through Sunday I would be at my real apartment in Halifax, a sublet I'd found online. The photos looked all right and the place got lots of sunlight, although the furniture was more traditional than my taste. But at least I'd have my urban fix to get me through the week.

"So, kiddo, I guess this is it for a while," Grant said.

When he called last night and invited me to dinner, I couldn't resist seeing him one last time, despite everything. After dinner, the wine kept flowing, followed by nightcaps and kisses and ravenous caresses which led to a kinky send-off, worthy of *Rome*. This morning I'd reclined on the chaise longue, while he ran around getting ingredients to make brunch, complete with mimosas, and the whole thing felt weirdly domestic.

Now we were sitting on barstools at the Rex Hotel, nursing our third gin and tonics. It was Sunday afternoon and the place was pretty deserted, aside from a bunch of grizzled old men finishing their second set. They were playing the blues, which suited my mood perfectly.

"Yeah, I guess this is it." I wondered if I meant "it" for good, or "it" until I got horny and needed another mood boost. But what was I thinking? In four days, I was heading back to the boonies.

"Oh, it won't be so bad," Grant said, leaning in to kiss me. "I'll come visit you in Halifax. I'll send you love letters."

"What if I meet someone in Halifax?"

"We'll find a way around it." He smiled, already excited at the prospect of a new game. "Hell, maybe I'll come visit you in Antigonish. Are there direct flights?"

I rolled my eyes. "Not unless you want to charter a helicopter."

"Sure, kiddo. Anything to see you."

My eyes misted, catching me off guard. Until this point, I hadn't felt much of anything for Grant, beyond camaraderie of the dysfunctional. But now I found tingles fluttering over my scalp and my stomach went hollow at the thought of not seeing him anymore.

We parted with one last kiss and I crossed Queen Street, wandering into the Condom Shack. I don't know why I went in – it wasn't like I needed to buy anything, except maybe a vibrator to get me through my stretch in Siberia.

Seriously, a vibrator wasn't a bad idea.

I walked to the back of the store and stared at the brightly coloured figurines, some moulded into weird shapes, others covered in a measles-like texture, and the most deluxe versions had flashing lights and whirring appendages. They were like effigies from some primitive, tribal culture, now degraded to the kitschiest of kitsch. So this was what my love life had come to.

A giggle escaped my lips, as I thought of the scene in *The Professor's House* where we get a glimpse of St. Peter's deranged sexuality. It's the scene where he's spending some quality time with the dressmaker's dummies in his attic. Years ago, the housekeeper left these dummies in the darkest corner and St. Peter has become perversely attached to one in particular. Whenever he's feeling down, he goes up to look at it, marvelling at its voluptuous bust. The headless, armless torso strangely excites him with its dead, inanimate quality and stirs his imagination in a way his wife no longer can.

And here I was, staring at fluorescent penis substitutes, no less of a perv than St. Peter.

Was this the endgame of the life of the mind?

"You might want to read this," Daddy said. He handed me a book with a grey cover entitled *Issei*.

I sat down on the sofa. "What is it?"

"Flip open to the Table of Contents. Your grandmother wrote something in it."

It was an anthology of personal and historical pieces that chronicled the accomplishments of the "early pioneers" in the Japanese-Canadian community. Sure enough, there was an essay called "Kozo Shimotakahara – First Japanese-Canadian Physician," by Granny.

"Kozo's story reminds me of Tom Outland's," Daddy said.

I smiled at my father's effort to engage with *The Professor's House,* but his claim seemed pretty far-fetched.

"I'm serious," he said.

"How do you mean?"

"Outland was a gifted student, an orphan who came from nowhere and did great things. So was Kozo."

I thought back to the scene where Tom Outland bursts into St. Peter's life. At first, St. Peter doesn't think much of him. Outland's just this kid dressed like a hick, a cowboy hat brimming his confident, eager face. He probably looked like some of the smarter students I'd taught, and I could relate to St. Peter's desire to get to know the kid, to take him under his wing, if only out of some deluded professorial vanity.

But little does he know that Outland is the real thing. Before he's even graduated, he makes a brilliant scientific discovery that leads to the development of a new aviation engine. Not bad for a boy from nowhere.

"But Kozo wasn't a self-taught genius," I said. "He had education."

"Not initially," Daddy said. "When he arrived in Canada at age fourteen, he barely even spoke English. He had to enroll in elementary school to learn his ABCs alongside little kids, while working as a houseboy for his room and board. His employers helped him along the way because they could see he had exceptional talents, like Outland. Granny writes about all this."

That night, when I couldn't sleep, I curled up on the sofa reading her essay. It was coming back to me now – the tone of idolatry in Granny's voice whenever she'd speak of my great-grandfather, extolling the way he'd cared for his people. Her essay chronicled all his acts of humanitarianism. After graduating from med school, Kozo set up his practice in Vancouver's Japantown, knowing that the community lacked a doctor. And he was such a saint that he provided his services free of charge to patients who couldn't afford to pay him. He toured the countryside showing films on tuberculosis to raise awareness among the Japanese-Canadian farming folk. He ran a blood drive to help his ailing colleague. And during the Second World War, Kozo served as the camp doctor at Kaslo for the meagre salary of one hundred dollars a month.

Reading about my ancestor's Messiah-like feats made me feel like I wasn't worthy of being his descendent.

I could feel the headache creeping up the back of my neck. I stiffened. It was infuriating to think about what I had to go back to – the academic politics, the petty squabbles about who got the latest grant. And as I looked ten or twenty years down the road, I couldn't see things getting any better. Even if I published a phonebook-sized oracle of leading-edge research and climbed the academic ladder like St. Peter, what did I really have to look forward to? The same ennui that had been grating on his soul for decades, slowly pushing him to a breakdown, was bound to get me in the end. There had to be more to the life of the mind, but why did everything seem so damn pointless?

By contrast to our pathetic lives, guys like Kozo and Outland were pretty amazing. They had something St. Peter and I would never have.

While we wasted our lives away in the lecture hall, these guys were actually out there *living*.

One rainy night, Outland tells St. Peter a story that lingers on in his imagination. It's a story about a summer he spent working as a cowhand and exploring a mesa on the Cruzados River, a massive blue rock of breathtaking beauty that no one had ever climbed before. Wending his way into the mesa, he discovers the remains of a Pueblo Indian community from ancient times. At first, it's just a few pieces of broken pottery, but then Outland starts finding whole pots, beautiful and intact, and at the core of the mesa is a perfectly designed stone city, frozen in time, like a city asleep. He even finds the desiccated body of a young woman whom he names "Mother Eve."

All the stresses of family and work fade away, as St. Peter contemplates this other civilization and imagines it as his own roots. His fascination and fantasy balloon into obsession, blotting out all reality. After a while he can barely function in his regular life.

As I mulled over his desperate desire to escape to the mesa, my thoughts drifted to Kozo. Granny's essay cast him as something of an explorer like Outland, chronicling the summers Kozo had spent as a fisherman's assistant in Steveston, where he'd managed to stay clear of all the gambling and drinking that messed the other men up. The lush landscape of British Columbia beckoned to Kozo and he felt like he'd finally found his true home.

That mysterious landscape emerged in my mind as my mesa.

What was it about these tales of exploration and long-lost origins? Just as St. Peter yearns to claim lineage from some elusive, primitive culture, everyone in my family idolized Kozo. It must have all started with the stories he'd told Granny, in much the way that Outland liked to confide in St. Peter. Those stories had taken on a life of their own in Granny's dreams, in all our dreams.

Maybe this was why I loved reading Cather – she understood the devastating homesickness of being cut off from your roots. The immigrant farming folk, who proved so inspirational to her early novels, had all but disappeared by the time she wrote *The Professor's House,* leaving nothing but gnawing anxiety.

She was depressed, dreadfully depressed, when she was writing this novel. Her prior novel, *One of Ours,* had won the Pulitzer Prize, elevating her to a level of fame that most writers can only dream of. But rather than being happy about her newfound celebrity – the requests for interviews, the countless letters from fans – Cather recoiled from the world. She hired a secretary to shield her from the public. In letters to friends, she complains of suffering from everything from neuritis and ringworm to back problems and a stiff neck. Or perhaps her deteriorating health was just a convenient excuse to stay in bed? I'd pulled that one before, too.

The fact that she was a lesbian living more or less in the closet – for more than forty years, she lived with her "companion," Edith Lewis – probably added to her sense of alienation. Cather dressed like a man and lusted after women, even though she never openly declared herself a lesbian like her contemporary Gertrude Stein.

Instead, she turned inwards. In much the way that St. Peter retreats from the world into the shelter of his fantasy life, so did Cather.

Was I, too, fated for loneliness and the dark crevices of my own mind?

I brushed plum shadow over my eyelids and stared at the face in the mirror. The colour was all wrong, but I didn't have time to change it. Tania was going to be here any minute. We were going to a party so I could meet her new friends, but I was already kicking myself for getting roped into going.

Tania was an old friend from high school. I'd run into her last week at Starbucks and she'd shrieked in delight, before telling me off for not calling her all summer. We exchanged numbers and I agreed to get together, but I'd been thinking a quiet glass of wine.

We sped down Yonge Street in her BMW, Tania talking non-stop about how busy she was. Her firm had recently promoted her to marketing director, so now she had to fly to trade shows all over the world. Paris, Hong Kong, Singapore. She had so many frequent flyer miles that she had no idea how she was ever going to spend them. She just might have to come visit me in my little town with the weird, long name.

As she prattled on, I slouched down in my seat. In the side mirror, my skin looked sallow, and that damn eye shadow was as attractive as a black eye. She, on the other hand, looked more stunning than ever, with her hair freshly bobbed and her complexion smooth as ivory.

"You're awfully quiet," she said suddenly.

It was pathetic how little we had in common now, but I couldn't expect her to know a thing about the Culture Wars or get excited about a new school pioneering neo-Marxist cultural studies.

"I'm just feeling stressed these days."

"No man in your life?"

I shook my head.

Tania flashed a smile. "There'll be lots of cute guys at this thing tonight. I'm going to introduce you to my friend, Per."

A tall guy with a shaved head and cryptic half-smile, Per turned out to be a DJ, and he claimed to do performance art on the side. He seemed to be enjoying his self-styled persona and not taking it too seriously. We were crammed against the railing of a crowded balcony outside a loft at College and Ossington. A couple of architects, Oliver and Nicholas, lived there.

Ambient music flowed onto the balcony, and inside I could see Tania making her rounds, slithering between dark-clad bodies, a flurry of scarves and kisses, clinking glasses. I was already on my third glass of wine, but I wasn't feeling any less morose or self-conscious. Well, the answer was obvious – another drink. What did it matter if I were hungover tomorrow? It would take the edge off packing.

As I fixed myself a gin and tonic, I thought about the dinner party scene in *The Professor's House,* where St. Peter just sits there for the whole evening, quietly observing everyone around him, basking in his own disapproving silence. The next morning, his wife accuses him of becoming intolerant and intolerable. A sudden terror washed over me. Was the same thing happening to me?

I walked back out onto the balcony and shoved my hand at the first person I saw standing alone. "Hi, I'm Leslie." Gin and tonic sloshed over as we tried to shake hands.

"Chris," he said, and continued to smoke his cigarette, inhaling deeply.

He was a tall, lanky, Asian guy dressed in black from head to toe. Black jeans and a well-structured jacket. His bangs swept over his forehead in a stylish wave, skimming the tops of his black glasses.

Normally, I was used to guys trying to chat me up, but this guy simply continued smoking. In a way, the silence was kind of nice. It made me feel not so abnormal.

Finally, I asked Chris how he knew the hosts, and he said that they all used to work together. But recently Chris and a couple of friends had started their own design studio, and he also taught part-time at University of Waterloo.

"Hey, I'm also a prof," I said. "English lit."

He looked up with interest. "What are you teaching next semester?"

I went through the syllabus for my Am Lit class, which became a springboard for a discussion about Hemingway. From there, we moved on to Walter Benjamin – one of the few philosophers who's influenced literary and architectural theory equally. I asked him what he was reading these days, and he said he'd just finished rereading *Architecture and Utopia* by Tafuri, because he was planning to teach it in his fall studio. Tafuri. I'd never heard of him and I was much too drunk to fake it. So I leaned forward on the balls of my feet – trying to get some circulation going after three hours in these strappy stilettos – and asked him if I could bum a smoke. Really, I just wanted an excuse to stand closer to him, as he cradled the flame and lit it for me, so I could get a better look at him. I knew I was pretty drunk by the way my perception of distances had faded, and maybe that was why everything he said sounded so interesting. I didn't normally go for well-dressed Asian guys, but this one had caught my attention.

"So what's this book by Tafuri about?" I asked.

"The death of architecture," he said, making a sweeping gesture. "Capitalism has rendered architecture obsolete. Now all we can do is revel in its sublime uselessness."

I was about to ask him what he meant by this delightfully provocative statement, when his phone rang. His friend had lost the address and was circling the block on his bike. Chris said he would be back in two minutes.

I wandered inside and fixed myself another drink.

Ten minutes went by. And another ten. People left and a stream of new faces arrived. But no Chris. He must have left, having forgotten all about me, not even thinking to come back for my email address.

I'd even lost the art of flirting.

I wanted to bury my head under the pillow, like Cather.

Slurping the rest of my drink, I slipped out the door without saying goodbye to anyone.

The next morning, Daddy asked if I wanted to see Granny one last time. I could tell that he didn't just mean one last time before going back to school. He meant the big "one last time." It was unlikely she'd be alive at Christmas.

Every time I saw her, her body looked a bit more shrivelled and brittle, but this time she barely seemed there at all. She didn't speak. She didn't open her eyes. Her flesh appeared to have dried up into a handful of bones and hair – eerily reminiscent of Mother Eve.

Daddy leaned over her, digital recorder in hand, but it was pointless to turn it on. His face appeared taut. Meanwhile, Aunt Wendy kept flitting around the room, checking monitors and calling out to the nurses, tears running down her cheeks. Even though she'd spent long nights by her mother's side, she needed more time to say all the things she wanted to say to her. But time was running out.

When I was growing up, Aunt Wendy had been my wild aunt. She used to have spiky hair and wear glittery purple and silver eye shadow and she was always gallivanting off to see Madonna and Cyndi Lauper concerts with her husband, Mike. Ten days after she'd given birth – by caesarean, no less – they went to see Michael Jackson. They threw big Christmas parties for which they rented karaoke machines, even though Aunt Wendy was the only one bopping her head and singing at the top of her lungs.

Back then, everyone loved Mike. He was a doctor. Aunt Wendy had realized Granny's dream of marrying a rich doctor.

Years later, after they'd divorced, Aunt Wendy became much more subdued. She did two years of psychotherapy and I remembered her telling my father that it was the best money she'd ever spent. Everyone in their family needed it, she said, staring at him for a long time. But Daddy scoffed. He wasn't reclining on any psychiatrist's couch or drawing Crayola pictures of his first house.

After a while, Daddy went to the cafeteria for coffee, but I decided to stay behind with Aunt Wendy.

"How do you think my father's handling all this?" I asked. "Do you think he's going to be okay?"

She pursed her lips and stared out the window. "I don't know. I've always thought Mom and Jack were so similar. I know he'd deny it, but it's the truth."

"How do you find them similar?"

"They both never talk about their feelings. They just keep everything bottled up."

"That's how they cope."

She nodded. "After our father had his first stroke, Jack moved out of the house. That was it – he packed up his stuff and just vanished. All he said was he needed to save himself. Man, was I jealous. I'd only just started high school, so I had to stay."

"Maybe that's why Daddy needs to ask Granny questions now," I said. "Since he wasn't around much, he needs to understand what happened."

Aunt Wendy rolled her eyes. "Don't you think there's something cruel about how he keeps interrogating her? If my own son tried that on my deathbed, I'd tell him to lay off for chrissakes."

"He just wants to understand Granny."

"But he *can't* understand her. He's got this frozen picture of Mom in his head. She's this cold, cruel woman who was never there for him when he was young."

"Are you saying his impression isn't true?"

Aunt Wendy shook her head and looked tired. "I'm just saying that memory is very subjective. Take, for instance, the way that Mom wrote about Kozo."

"She makes him into a bloody saint."

"And he wasn't."

Chills fluttered over my shoulders. "He wasn't?"

"I'm not disputing that Kozo was a brilliant doctor and had a hell of a work ethic, but he also had a darker side. He was a terrible perfectionist and if people didn't come up to his standards, he flew into a rage. More than once, he threw his wife down the basement stairs. And Mom was there."

I turned away, hostility spreading warmly across my chest. I didn't want it to be true. Why did she have to ruin my view of my one good ancestor, my Tom Outland?

"Then why did Granny write about Kozo so glowingly?"

Aunt Wendy looked at me warily, gauging how much to say. "Let's just say that Mom had a hard childhood. Her mother was away in Japan for much of the time, and her father wasn't the nicest man. That's why she was never able to be maternal – she didn't know what it's like to come from a stable family. When she met Kaz's family, Kozo must have appeared in her mind as the ideal father she'd never had. He was a doctor and a leader in the community. That was all that mattered to her. She didn't see the rest of the man."

Tears smarted in my eyes. What she was saying made sense on a rational level, yet in my gut I couldn't believe it. I wanted to hang on to my image of my heroic ancestor, and nothing she could say would take that desire away.

Two more days before I had to go back. Every bone in my body ached as I heaved a last load of laundry into the dryer. Sharp pains shot up my wrists into my shoulders and neck. My chest tightened every time I thought about getting on the plane. Cramps cut across my abdomen and it was nowhere close to that time of the month.

There had to be something wrong with me. I had to see my doctor.

Dr. Bernstein had been my physician since my teenage years and I usually felt calmed just being in her presence, feeling the cool stethoscope against my back. Today, however, it was obvious that she was in a rush and perplexed as to why I was there at all.

"I don't know what's wrong with me," I said. "My body feels sluggish one minute, and the next minute I'm on a bed of pins."

"How have you been sleeping?"

"Dreadful. Weird, cinematic dreams. I wake up sweating, feeling like I've just stepped out of *The Shining*."

"Are you under a lot of stress?"

I nodded, and she waited for me to explain. But I couldn't explain. With her waiting room full of crying babies and arthritic old women, was she going to be at all sympathetic to my woes? Fat chance. Like my dad, she'd think I had it easy – the life of the mind, reading all day on the couch.

"Well, I have to tell you," she said, "I can't find anything wrong. Maybe you should try exercise. Yoga might be good."

I perched on the edge of the exam table and stared at the dry, powdery skin on my feet. *She couldn't find anything wrong with me. There was nothing wrong with me – except that I felt like I was dying. Death was everywhere in my life.*

After Dr. Bernstein had left the room, I curled up in a ball in the corner of the exam table and hugged the stiff grey sheet around me, my mind drifting to the scene at the end of *The Professor's House* where St. Peter goes to the doctor. Like me, he's told there's nothing wrong with him. No wonder people thought academics were a bunch of wimpy hypochondriacs.

St. Peter continues teaching and trudging through his daily routines, but the sensation that death is around the corner never fades. By this point, Tom Outland is dead, leaving the professor feeling that the most vital part of himself is dead. And what else is there to live for anyway?

One evening, he falls asleep in his study and narrowly escapes dying from a gas leak. But the strange thing is he's aware of what's happening and does nothing to save himself. He just can't find the strength to go on.

Nor could I. I remained curled up in the fetal position, until a nurse banged on the door.

chapter ten

What impressed him that time, he even mentioned it later, cool he called
it, was the way I took off my clothes and put them on again later very
smoothly as if I were feeling no emotion. But I really wasn't.
                                              -Margaret Atwood, *Surfacing*

I couldn't believe I was on this bus again. The chemical-sweet smell of the
blue liquid in the toilet, swishing back and forth in time to our lurches,
mixing with the smell of feet.

But this bus was the only way to get from Halifax to Antigonish. So for
the next two and a half hours, I was trapped beside an old lady with rancid
hair.

Through the window, everything looked grey as the inside of a steel
plant. Halifax's industrial shoreline. It started to rain, lightly at first, then
heavily. I pressed my nose against the glass. An old man pushing a shopping
cart full of waterlogged bags stirred my sympathy and I wanted to plead
with the driver to let him on.

But of course I just sat there, a book on my lap. Terrified that the girl
across the aisle would be one of my students.

After we passed Truro, the land opened up. The bungalows and cheap suburban dwellings gave way to countryside – wide expanse, hulking barns like giant shipwrecks, white farmhouses dotting the horizon, bales of hay, real live cows. Time stopped, even as we sped past. The only signs of modern life were billboards for McDonalds and KFC, marking the next exit for the grease-starved.

I wondered what kind of people lived here. I tried to imagine being a child and running across the fields, making dandelion bouquets and conjuring up woodland fairies, but all I could see were the artificially rosy cheeks of kids from TV. Ads for allergy pills and antidepressants.

The novel lying open on my lap was *Surfacing* by Margaret Atwood. I'd grabbed it off my mother's bookshelf before Daddy drove me to the airport. I had a vague memory of having read it as a child. The sex scenes had intrigued me. These were my clandestine thrills as a curious pre-teen – one day Atwood, the next day Danielle Steel. The high and the low occupied a level plane on my mother's bookshelves, but I quickly discovered my own preference for the darkness and power games and animal-like perversion that characterize Atwood's best novels.

My eyes flitted from the typeset words to the trickling raindrops, and I had the queer sensation of slipping into the novel. The opening pages are about an unnamed narrator's return home to an isolated region in northern Quebec. Packed into a jalopy with her lover, Joe, and their friends, Anna and David, she observes the vestiges of civilization slipping by – "an accumulation of sheds and boxes and one main street with a movie theatre, the itz, the oyal, red R burnt out." Terror and a diffuse sense of something invading her home territory come over her; she notes signs of rich Americans and the white birch trees now diseased.

She's going to a place where eccentric types like her father come to be alone, living in a self-imposed, mysterious exile. The purpose of her trip is to find her father on the island, where he's vanished. She worries he's ended up mired in the black spruce swamp.

I, too, was crossing the threshold into the boondocks. Beyond which lay the wilderness and the wilderness within.

While growing up in this area, the narrator and her family were always outsiders – interlopers to this francophone region, the evil *anglais*. The place could never be "home" to her, any more than Antigonish could be home to me.

And yet, Toronto also didn't feel like home anymore.

So here I was sitting on this bus, feeling as if I wasn't going anywhere, just drifting, lurching along, my chest tightening with every bump.

The sea of faces. Sweat dripping off the end of my nose. Everything passed by in a blur, as I handed out syllabuses and avoided eye contact and stared ahead at the windowless cement walls of the lecture hall, the green paint reminiscent of my grandmother's death chamber.

It might as well be my own. Another thirty years of looking at this wall.

How strange it was to hear myself launching into the lecture – the cheeriness in my voice so forced, so brittle. The notes I'd slaved over last year were now dog-eared, ringed with coffee. How the hell was I supposed to make sense of this late-night jumble? I had no clue what I'd been thinking back then. Back then, I'd been bright-eyed and bushy-tailed and high on the exhilaration of bearing the title "Dr." But now, I was barely able to string together a coherent sentence and *what had I been on when I wrote this crap anyway?* But as my pulse galloped, I just kept talking, my voice taking on an automatic rhythm, and all the while I was imagining I was that zoned-out kid at the back of the class, head bent, iPod earpieces jammed into her ears. Praying for the fifty minutes to be up.

What did it matter how I performed anyway? These kids had already voted me the Worst Prof Ever.

But this time around I wasn't going to make the mistake of asking questions in hopes of provoking any kind of discussion. No more eerie silences. Every second would be filled with the prattle of my own voice, nonsensical bullet points shooting out at two hundred kilometres an hour, like a train run off its tracks.

Every Monday afternoon, after arriving by bus, I would drag my suitcase to the edge of campus and up a muddy hill that led to Mrs. Lewis' house. Mrs. Lewis was our landlady, a white-haired dame with a tight smile. She lived alone in a white clapboard house with a host of angels – figurines, cheap oil paintings and posters of chubby cherubs covered every wall and surface. Beatific sayings like "The Lord sent an angel, He sent you my way!" were plastered everywhere, hovering above little dishes of candy.

The basement where Ben and I lived consisted of two small bedrooms and a rec room with wood panelling and motheaten plaid sofas. Pipes ran across the ceilings. A tiny window in the corner of my room afforded a slip of light from the driveway. There was no kitchen in our basement. Nor did we have kitchen privileges, but at least we were allowed our own microwave and fridge.

The first few nights, Ben and I sat around in our bathrobes drinking beer and munching on pizza pockets, but the smell of mildew killed my appetite. Soon, we started eating in our offices. It was a strange, rootless life.

I was in my office one night marking papers, when Daddy called.

"What are you reading?" he asked, his voice groggy.

The clock on my desk said 1:32. "Shouldn't you be asleep?"

But weird dreams had been plaguing his mind. All he could remember upon waking up was an image of the house on St. Clarens, the murky air of the basement.

I told him I hadn't had time to read much of anything lately. *Surfacing* was the last book I'd read for pleasure. When he asked if I'd recommend it, I hesitated. Few men, in my experience, like Atwood and those that do are usually Can Lit scholars. But I could hear the thirst for something – anything – in his voice, so I started telling him about the novel, simplifying its complex psychological dynamics, paring it down to the bare bones of its plot.

"It's basically a story about a man who's vanished in the bush," he said approvingly.

"Yeah," I said, biting my tongue. It was too late to get into it with him. Even though a part of me wanted to get into it. *Surfacing* isn't just a story about a man vanishing in the bush. Duh. The narrator's real terror is that her old man's gone stark raving mad. And in following him to the island of his final retreat, she feels herself slipping over the edge, while the animal world beckons to her. She feels herself sprouting leaves, growing antlers. *Madness*. Father and daughter are both hovering on the brink of madness, bound by their elusive quests.

I wanted to say that I identified all too well with the Atwood narrator. Again, I bit my tongue.

"Well, this novel sounds rather good," Daddy said. "I'll read it. Your mother should have a copy on her bookshelf, right?"

"I don't know if she has it anymore. It's an old novel – I think she sent it to the Salvation Army a couple of decades ago." My cheeks flushed. Why didn't I just say I'd taken it with me? But my father could get feisty about things leaving his house.

He said he'd get it from the library.

"You should."

Maybe reading it would help him understand me. Parallels between myself and the miserable narrator sprung forth in my mind.

Years ago, the narrator had dreamed of being an artist, but after a professor told her there had never been any great female artists, she resigned herself to commercial work. So she illustrates children's books and makes posters and advertisements, thankful to have a steady paycheque, but all the while she bristles at having sold out on her childhood dream.

Rudderless, we both were. I, too, was paying the price for turning my back on the one thing I loved.

Similarities between Daddy and the narrator's dad also filled my mind. There were times when I worried my father was going to die in some unimaginable accident of his own making or better yet, go insane. He was a man who loved to take chances. When he used to travel on business in Africa and South America, he'd send us pictures of himself sitting at bars in godforsaken parts of town and hiking across all too rugged landscapes. I could see him going off on a journey to the wilderness for vague reasons – what was it about the wilderness that called out to men's souls?

But more than simply the call of the wild, it turns out that what has consumed the narrator's father is an obsession with roots. She discovers in his desk cryptic drawings of stick figures and faceless faces with branches for ears that she at first sees as signs of mania. It turns out, however, that these sketches are based on crude drawings he's seen on nearby rocks; he devoted his final days to documenting the primitive tribe that once inhabited the area. At the end of his life, his imagination circled back to the beginning, the *very* beginning. Like St. Peter and Tom Outland, he wanted to penetrate the mystery of our primal origins – man in pure nature, before culture, before anything.

These sketches brought to mind my own father's project to record my grandmother's feeble, dying voice. Daddy's behaviour became less baffling as I thought about how he, too, was obsessed with understanding that dark place from which he'd come.

I only hoped that he didn't wander too far and, like the narrator's father, fall into the water to his icy death.

Daddy interrupted my thoughts. "Did you know that Kozo also disappeared in the bush?"

"He did?"

"Yeah, Granny wrote about it."

He said that in the decades after the war, Kozo had become increasingly depressed about his inability to rebuild his medical practice. Kaslo emerged in his mind as the place where everything had gone wrong; he felt he was being punished for some sin he'd committed. Daddy speculated he was plagued by guilt over his role as the camp doctor, regretting that he'd assisted in the internment of his own people. What else could have compelled him to return to Kaslo? A feeble old man, he insisted on moving back all alone to the ghost town, like he was doing penance. He envisioned Kaslo as the only place where his practice could begin afresh. Despite his family's attempts to stop him, he was adamant about going back.

But no Japanese-Canadians lived in Kaslo anymore, so his only patients were phantoms of days gone by. The harsh weather took a toll on his health.

One day, a couple of motorists found poor Kozo wandering by the side of the road – dazed and covered in scrapes and bruises, rambling on in some indecipherable language, not Japanese, not English, his hair matted with leaves. Days earlier, he'd crashed his car into the trees, while driving to see one of his imaginary patients. He'd been foraging in the ground for food and sleeping in his car for God knows how long.

Shortly after, he had a stroke and died.

Daddy's voice trembled with horror and glee as he told the story and I had a sudden image of him, ten years older, wandering in a daze on the side of the road. It ran in our family, this unhealthy obsession with the past.

The damp chill of fall was seeping into my bones, a numb bruise spreading across my back.

Josh kept emailing me, but I brushed him off. At first, I told him I was up to my eyeballs in marking. But deep down I wanted him to know that I was onto his games.

"How's the missus?" I typed. "Maybe the next time I'm in New York for a conference, the three of us can have brunch."

"She's very shy," he wrote back – not even mentioning his wife's name or asking how I'd found out about her. "I don't think she'd enjoy herself. But we can have brunch."

I tried to think of a witty reply to show him that his marriage was nothing but a big joke to me, but my mind was a black sea. Trite, angry words were all that came to me. So I just didn't write back.

After a while, he stopped trying to contact me and I felt worse than ever.

Whenever I became sad and stressed out, all the old symptoms came back with a vengeance. Dark thoughts about Dr. Foote clouded my mind: his pudgy hands, his sweaty cheeks, his sad, grandfatherly smile. The thoughts became more frequent – daily, hourly – as the weather got colder and every step sent pangs into my hips.

It was as though the brace were still hugging my ribcage, contracting my lungs. I couldn't breathe as I raced from my office to the lecture hall and back again, file folders spilling from my arms, and my breath grew shallower and shallower as my pulse hammered in my head and I recoiled from students calling me "Dr. Shimo" and "Professor," their faces alight with grand expectations. The leather buckles pulled the fibreglass tight around me, so tight that every time I took a tiny gulp of air my ribs seemed to quiver and I could still feel those straps constricting me and I could still see those dark patches of discoloured skin.

My whole life had become my brace. I was trapped between the fibreglass walls of Antigonowhere.

Lights glimmered across the harbour. I was standing in the kitchen, a wine glass in hand, feeling like I ought to be uncorking another bottle or preparing an appetizer, but all I could do was stare out the window, as the cheery voices hemmed me in.

I felt like a grade-A hypocrite for being here at all. But when Bobby came up behind me and locked his arms around my waist, I didn't squirm away.

This was the first party we were appearing at together. This made it official: everyone would think we were back together.

Don't get me wrong, I still despised him. Yet here we were. When I'd run into Bobby at the supermarket a few weeks ago, much to my surprise, I hadn't blown him off. As he inched closer to me, smiling mischievously, I'd smiled and flirted back. The truth was that I was glad to see him – thrilled, actually. Who else was I supposed to hang out with? I enjoyed riding around town on the back of his motorcycle, and most of all I loved attracting the shocked stares of faculty, particularly faculty in the Catholic Studies department.

Years ago, the Catholics had branded Bobby the biggest womanizer in town. What a joke. Over the past ten years, he might have dated all of three women, but his sin was that he'd failed to propose to any of them. And since one of his ex-girlfriends had been the dentist's daughter, he was persona non grata indeed. Rumours about his sadistic sexual habits and predilection for *ménage à trois* abounded, along with rumours he used a sunlamp to grow pot.

If only. He was the squarest, most meat-and-potatoes guy I'd dated in my life.

Clark was hosting the party tonight. He was Bobby's neighbour; they shared the same strip of beachfront, although Clark owned four times as much property. He'd made a bundle flipping houses in Toronto, before his divorce a number of years ago, and now he just wanted to get away from it all, a strangely decadent exile. The house he'd built was a massive, modern chalet, replete with glass walls that scandalized the locals by providing a glimpse of him walking around in the buff. A half-dozen cottages surrounded his house. Clark rented them to rich American tourists in the summer.

Yeah, Clark was a character. If he hadn't been shorter than me, I might have tried to date him myself.

The people who were at this party were a very mixed bag. Most of Clark's friends seemed to be ex-girlfriends from Halifax – divorcees wearing too much makeup and bearing heaping casseroles, all too eager to stay late to do the dishes. And then there were his winter tenants, a smattering of misfits who rented the cottages in the off-season for next to nothing. Jupiter, for instance, was a white-bearded gentleman who said he was an astrologer for some tabloid in London. He loved how clear the night sky was out here. This was his retreat to help realign his energies with the orbits.

"So what's in the stars for me?" I asked.

He closed his eyes like he was really concentrating. "I'm detecting a lot of turbulent energy around you. The next year is going to be full of upheaval."

Great. Just what I needed to hear.

Standing beside Jupiter was a pretty blonde girl who looked strikingly similar to Jodie Foster in *Taxi Driver.* She was wearing tight blue jeans and go-go boots and a black beret pulled over her bleached curls. I wondered if she was a university student, but she looked barely old enough to be in high school.

"I'm Vivian," she said. But there was something about the way her eyes fluttered and looked askance that made me think that wasn't her real name. Her real name was probably Jane or Mary.

"God, I'm so bored at this party," she said, helping herself to a double vodka.

"Tell me about it."

"I like your earrings. Where did you get them?" She leaned toward me and her fingertips brushed the silver strands and I caught a whiff of drugstore perfume. *Charlie* or something. The kind I used to wear back in junior high.

When I said that I got my earrings at the One of a Kind Show in Toronto, her face lit up. She'd never been to Toronto, but she hoped to move there eventually. The city – "the Big Smoke," as she kept calling it – was the only place where a girl could get a decent paying job. And she needed a good job if she was ever going to convince that stupid social worker to give her kids back. Her youngest had just turned two.

"Where do you work now?" I asked.

"I change old folks' diapers at the home, on the days they need extra help. It doesn't pay much, but Jupiter's been taking care of me." She slipped her arm around his thick waist.

So they were a couple. Back in grad school, I'd dated a professor twenty years my senior, but this astrologer had to be at least *sixty* years Vivian's senior. The thought of the two of them naked together turned my stomach.

Bobby came in carrying a tray of grilled burgers. "Hey, babe, what are you doing talking to the riffraff?" He slapped Jupiter on the back, practically knocking the old guy over. "You've got to meet Clark's new woman, Jillian. She's also a snob from Toronto."

Across the room, a blonde woman flashed Bobby a smile. From a distance, Jillian looked like she might be in her late thirties, but up close it became evident she had to be closer to fifty. She chattered on non-stop about herself – her personal trainer, her love of yoga. Her career as an accountant had proved so lucrative she was headed for early retirement.

"Hey," Bobby interrupted, "did you know these guys hooked up on Lavalife? Thanks to Internet dating, the universe really is getting smaller."

But if this was the first time Jillian was meeting Clark in the flesh, their first date didn't appear to be going well. Everyone could see him across the room flirting with his ex, Tammy.

"You actually flew all the way out here to go on a date?" I said.

A sheen of insecurity came across her face and I regretted opening my big mouth. But the damage was done. Her smile turned to pure cattiness, powder caked into her laugh lines.

"You actually moved out here to take a job?" she said.

"The academic job market's in the toilet."

She stared disdainfully out the window at the dense trees and pulled her shawl tighter. "Well, maybe you ought to consider another line of work. I'd go crazy if I had to live in the bush."

I was surprised that my first instinct was to defend this beautiful backwater. Whatever. I didn't want to admit it, yet she was right – I *was* on the verge of going crazy.

But I was in no mood to take advice from a bitch from Toronto.

In October, Grant came to visit me in Halifax. I greeted him at the door of my new apartment dressed in a schoolgirl costume I'd bought just for the occasion, martini shaker in hand. He was all over me in two seconds flat and the old primal sensations flooded back.

An hour later, we lay on the crumpled sheets, as he murmured tender, dirty words in my ear.

And yet, something was off-kilter. I wasn't used to feeling so much . . . *feeling.* Now that Josh was out of the picture, now that that door had finally been slammed shut, I found all my emotions loose and aimless.

But what was I thinking in getting attached to Grant?

We got half dressed and went onto the balcony, where we leaned against the railing, smoking cigarette after cigarette, the smoke mixing with the fog and mist. Halifax Harbour shone in the distance.

Grant was wearing a faded "I ♥ NY" T-shirt – who would have guessed that under his tailor-made shirt, this was his grubby undershirt? The big fat heart reminded me of a throbbing cock. That was basically what he was to me, I reminded myself.

I dragged heavily on my smoke and stared out at the horizon.

Was I becoming horribly cynical like the narrator in *Surfacing?* At times like this, I identified all too well with her cool remove. When she first meets

Joe at the hardware store, it doesn't take long for her to slip her clothes off with such ease – such perfect thoughtlessness – that he later comments on her lack of emotion. But what first strikes him as exciting and carefree soon begins to grate on his soul. Men were like that. They pretended to want no strings attached, but deep down they wanted you to try to trap them in a domestic cage. What a shock to discover that some women really do want no strings. How I could relate to her claustrophobia. A similar tightness had been gripping my chest.

I felt it every time Bobby looked at me – so possessive, so sure of himself. He was forty. He was ready to settle down, and who but a hardened city girl like myself would be willing to give the town womanizer a second chance?

I hated how he assumed I was staying. Sooner or later, he figured, I would have to get over my airs. It was only a matter of time before I'd be forced to take stock of my options and settle.

Grant was my out, my safety valve. Every time we fucked, it was an exhilarating reminder that I wasn't going to rot my life away in that town.

Around eleven, we went out to a little bistro, where we feasted on seafood bisque and homemade biscuits and drank a bottle of wine with hints of green apple.

"So, Luffle," he said, leaning across the table. (Luffle was his nickname for me – I had no idea how he'd come up with it). "When are you going to move home? I'm love-starved without you."

He was full of bullshit. And yet, it was exactly what I wanted to hear.

Bobby saw an ad for a rowboat in the local paper. He asked if I wanted to come with him to check it out one day after work. His idea of a fun date.

I could use a boat. A lifeboat. But what else was I supposed to do with myself on a Wednesday evening?

Bobby's hand resting on my knee, I watched the landscape speed by. The trees had turned burnt orange and golden yellow and for a moment I got lost in the rolling hills, dotted with houses that seemed to vanish into the landscape. As we got closer to the coast, the houses appeared larger and more interesting architecturally; they had bay windows and octagonal towers of the kind that had caught my fancy as a little girl when I'd imagined myself as Rapunzel. Yet the paint was peeling and the windows were boarded or smashed. The only signs of life were at the gas station, where a grizzled old man sat outside making bait.

Vivian had mentioned she was from a fishing village that made Antigonish look like Manhattan. No wonder she'd hightailed it and shacked up with Jupiter.

"These houses go for a song," Bobby said. "When the owners die, their kids sell off everything all for one price – right down to the furniture and cutlery. I'd love to pick one up right along the water. Don't you think that would be nice?"

I smiled and tried to control the gerbil scaling the walls of my stomach. *Like hell was I sleeping on some dead lady's sheets.* It would be like living in the house in *Psycho.*

He parked in front of a big white shed with a hand-painted sign: "Marina." An old man in overalls ambled out and Bobby greeted him with a hearty handshake, even as the man looked at him warily. There was something almost touching about Bobby's desire to create community and pretend that anyone could belong here, if you just walked tall. Could he really be oblivious to the fact that people were constantly shunning him?

While they trudged to the dock negotiating a price, I stood at the edge of the road. The heels of my boots were sinking into the dirt. The purple clouds, shot through with the last bit of sun, lighting up the craggy shoreline, were fascinating in a painterly way, yet all this beauty oppressed me.

I didn't want to be trapped in a goddamned painting.

On the drive back, Bobby chattered about his weekend in Halifax – he wanted to know why I'd been MIA. He'd gone to visit some friends in the city and thought we could all hang out. But when he'd called me, I hadn't even answered my phone.

My cheeks flushed, a wave of guilt. My dirty weekend with Grant. My pleasure pill.

"Oh, I must have been busy marking papers."

"So I was having a few beers with my old school friend, Dave," Bobby continued, "and we were at this packed bar on Argyle Street. It was full of hot chicks, but the strange thing was they were all really young or really old. Some of them were nineteen, dancing their asses off, and the others were, like, fifty, standing by the wall sipping martinis. My buddy and I couldn't get over it. We were like, where are all the hot early-thirties women who have good jobs but are still young enough to spit out babies?" He looked at me meaningfully.

"Shucks, I guess they're all taken."

He continued looking at me seriously. "Don't you ever think about settling down?"

"Here?"

He nodded.

I shook my head. "As I've told you before, I'm not staying."

"That so?" he said, his cheeks reddening. "Everyone here at some point said they're leaving, but how many people do you think actually do it? Do you think I planned to spend my life here? I started on an eight-month contract."

The anger in his voice frightened me, and his driving was becoming erratic. Nausea gripped my stomach.

"Stop the car," I said.

"What are you talking about?"

"Stop the car – I'm going to be sick!"

Bobby pulled over beside a field and I jumped out, leaning over, hands on my knees, my stomach a whirlpool of grief. I gagged and coughed but nothing came up. I wanted to barf up my life – but I just kept dry heaving.

I stared at the dark forest beyond the field and I could feel everything folding back into that primitive, atavistic world that Atwood depicts so beautifully in *Surfacing*. I sympathized all too well with the narrator's misery, her loss of grip on reality, as she feels herself returning to the animal kingdom and the struggle for bare survival. It turns out in the end that her lack of affect, her inability to feel much of anything, is more than just a personality trait. She had a humiliating love affair, which culminated in an abortion. She suffered a breakdown. The cleft she now feels through her entire body was painfully familiar, for I, too, knew what it felt like to pass under the surgeon's knife and never be the same. And it was more than just my back tormenting me now. It was more than just a man, or string of men, who had disappointed me again and again.

I was coming to realize that the biggest blow to my ego was my loss of vocation. Cheesy as it sounded, that was what my career as an English professor was supposed to be. More than just a career. A *vocation*. Over the years, I'd built it up in my mind as some sacred relationship with the world of letters, my point of communion with that body of dead, beloved authors who would always hold the greatest allure for me. I'd sacrificed everything to become a Doctor of Philosophy, to bear the letters "Ph.D." after my name, and where had it gotten me? I felt so tired and jaded I simply couldn't bear to go on. My dream was a fuck-up. What could possibly replace it now?

Would I always be a miserable failure in my father's eyes?

I wondered if Kozo had felt so devastated – so cheated – when he returned to Kaslo at the end of his life. I pictured him trudging along the deserted road, bloody and filthy, his clothes torn, baffled by where he had veered off course, tormented by his realization that it was all too late. Lost in the bush.

I was also lost in my own dark thoughts, my endless musings about where I'd taken a wrong turn, and if I let myself, I might never find my way out of this wilderness.

I looked over at Bobby, his puzzled, annoyed face, and almost felt a pang of tenderness. "I'm sorry. I just want to go home."

His confusion sharpened into a scowl. "You're a long way from home, city girl."

Back in Mrs. Lewis' basement, I stood in front of the fridge for a long time, the light illuminating the damp grey carpet. Cold was gnawing at my stomach, but the effort of unwrapping and microwaving a slab of chicken and rice seemed hardly worth the tasteless morsels. Finally, I opened one of Ben's fruit cups and ate the syrupy pineapple chunks with my fingers. I was thinking of a scene in the novel where the narrator eats canned beans with her fingers and then digs in the dirt for carrots, giving in completely to the sensation of becoming a wild animal. By this point, she's all alone on the island. Joe and their friends had left on the boat at the appointed time, while she hid in the brush, intent on being alone and returning to nature. But her aloneness suddenly closes in on her. Far from offering some beautiful freedom, the wilderness brings her face to face with the darkness in her head. The world has deserted her. Even the dead flowers seem to have died just to get away from her. She calls out into the empty air, but there's no one to take pity on her.

"I'm here," I hissed, imitating her futile gesture.

It was my parents and friends and lovers and ex-lovers I was calling out to, at the same time loathing them for being able to carry on with their merry lives while I remained trapped in this musty basement.

Wandering into my room, I perched on the cot, looking at the water stains on the particleboard ceiling, disgusted at the thought of taking my shoes off. I had even stopped unpacking each week; my suitcase lay open on the floor, a hodgepodge of turtlenecks and novels. And what was I doing lugging around all these folders full of research notes and photocopies from rare-book libraries? They were my research files from back in the days when I was working on my dissertation, and although it had been years since I'd seriously worked on the project, I clung to the fantasy that I was fast at work turning it into a book manuscript. The folders weighed down my suitcase like a load of cement, killing my shoulders every time I came here. But each week something compelled me to stick to the ritual, which marked my identity as a rising scholar.

Time to give up the charade.

I listened to the rain pattering against my little window. My cheeks grew hot with anger. The words of my mentors echoed in my ears – "You've got to stick out the hard times at the beginning of your career," "Stay the course," "You've got star potential" – and all of it suddenly rang hollow. I hated those notes and wanted them out of my sight immediately – or better still, let me tear them to shreds. Down on all fours, like a starved animal, I rummaged through the folders, spewing out the papers, a bath of illegible print, covered in highlighter and sticky notes. Even my handwriting looked different back then – tightly curled, in control. It shocked me that I could barely recognize my own writing.

All the old feelings of devastation were coming back now, feelings that went back to before I'd even contemplated doing a Ph.D. I'd learned early that sticking it out didn't always lead to the desired result. I remembered being perched on the edge of the exam table, teetering, about to fall off, when Dr. Foote breezed in wearing his sad smile. The brace hadn't succeeded in halting the curve, he announced, so surgery would be necessary and we had to act fast. The curve was rapidly getting worse.

But there I was again, a year later, as he showed us a new set of post-surgery X-rays. The bright white screen illuminated all the hardware now attached to my spine, all the nails and screws and splints, and if seeing that didn't make it real enough, I had the twelve-inch scar running numb along my side to remind me. Dr. Foote was taking care to keep his voice soft and gentle as he explained to my mother that after surgery, it was possible for the curve to revert to how it was before the operation. This was what had happened to me.

Subtle ringing filled my ears and everything in the room appeared to be trembling. "So it was all for nothing!"

"No, you're still better off," Dr. Foote said. "At least your spine's stopped moving. It's unlikely to get worse."

I stared at the X-ray of my spine still curving like an S, with the useless rod now attached – looking like a stretched thin, lopsided dollar sign. It was absurd and infuriating, and the worst part of it all was that I was expected to play along with the charade that this was somehow a successful outcome. But I couldn't smile and thank my surgeon for all he'd done for me. Words, harsh words, were flying from my lips and I didn't even know what I was saying and I couldn't stop crying, to the point that my cheeks went numb and my words unravelled into guttural cries, while Dr. Foote looked out the window, his cheeks turning to storm clouds.

It must have been at that moment that I lost faith in sticking it out.

And now I wanted to destroy everything about my sorry-ass life in the way that the narrator in *Surfacing* throws her paintbrushes and jars of paint and half-assed drawings into the fire, along with a cheap ring from the man who broke her heart.

Fire purifies. It symbolizes that she's walking away from her miserable career and twisted love life and anaesthetized body – finally moving on.

The most famous lines of the novel rung in my ears: "This above all, to refuse to be a victim. Unless I can do that I can do nothing."

I, too, wanted to refuse to be a victim. I wanted to move on, but move on to *what*? I had no friggin' idea.

I gathered up the folders and ran outside to the dumpster behind Mrs. Lewis' house, rain gushing onto my cheeks, adrenalin coursing through my veins.

One, two, three. . . . Hadn't I read somewhere that Atwood had thrown in the towel on her own dissertation on Victorian literature?

I let go and heard the pages cascading over the edge onto the garbage bags below.

The half-moon smiled down and calmness suddenly came over me. I just stood there, letting the rain soak through to my underwear.

chapter eleven

Who knows but that, on the lower frequencies, I speak for you?

-Ralph Ellison, *Invisible Man*

The fluorescent lights reflected off the sweat on my cheeks. I was standing at the front of the lecture hall, *Invisible Man* tucked in my armpit. Yellow sticky papers fanned out, but somehow I couldn't even manage to make it to the first quote.

"Why does our narrator refer to himself as an 'Invisible Man'?" I asked. "What does he mean in claiming to be invisible?"

Dead silence. Everyone stared down at their laptops and iPhones. Text messages shot around the room.

So I pretended to be the most enthusiastic student in the class, my hand shooting up, eager to explain that our nameless narrator is talking about a kind of social invisibility foisted upon him, simply by virtue of his skin colour. Writing in the 1940s and '50s, I explained, Ralph Ellison was all too aware of the black stereotypes alive in the cultural imagination, and it's these stereotypes he's confronting and combatting in his novel.

"Do you get what I'm talking about?"

More blank gazes. I stared out at the sea of blonde heads and peaches-

and-cream complexions and the irony that I was the only non-white person in the room hit me with a dull chuckle.

"Throughout the novel," I continued, "we see Ellison using a slew of black stereotypes, but he never uses them simply as they are – he reconfigures them in creative ways."

A few students looked interested, but most seemed to be struggling to stay awake. But who could blame them? I also desperately wanted the lecture to be over and we were only five minutes into the period.

Time to spell things out. "Let's look at a concrete example. In chapter two, Ellison ingeniously calls upon black stereotypes – the folk farmer who's sleeping with his daughter, for example – but he uses these stereotypes in such innovative ways that they cease to be simply stereotypes. They become fodder for Jim Trueblood's original storytelling mode. As we, along with the Invisible Man, listen to Trueblood telling his story, we come to see him as something more than just a folk farmer – we come to see him as having a unique interiority."

"What's a unique interiority?" a kid at the back called out.

My cheeks flushed. I hated being caught off-guard like this. What a hypocrite I was. I told myself I wanted student participation, but the truth was I found it terrifying being challenged on the spot. I hadn't anticipated having to define this term and now there were forty pairs of eyes glued on me. After a deadly silence, I managed to launch into a monologue about psychoanalytic theory, knowing full well that not a soul in the room would understand a word I was saying.

The days were getting shorter. The icy chill seeped into my bones, a blanket of aches. My lips cracked and bled. All weekend I stayed in bed, living off microwave popcorn and Neo-Citran, old movies starring Judy Garland playing in the background (one of the networks was doing a tribute), and all I could think was how much I wanted to click my ruby slippers and repeat,

"There's no place like home."

I couldn't continue on in this dead-end life. But where was my magical exit strategy?

Monday morning rolled around and I kept lying in bed, even though I knew I had to catch the bus to the university in less than an hour.

Finally, I emailed my class saying I'd been bowled over by some mysterious virus and would be recuperating for the rest of the week. Mischievous glee fluttered over me as I climbed back under the covers. The students weren't the only ones who could play hooky.

But it didn't take long for my relief to turn back to anxiety. What the fuck was I doing with my life?

Harriet and I were back to our regular therapy sessions, but it often seemed she needed help more than I did. Why did she get so excited whenever I told her that Grant had sent me another love letter or come to town for a dirty weekend? Grant was no good for me – that seemed obvious enough – so shouldn't she be pushing me toward recognizing that he had to go? But instead she seemed to be relishing how much attention I received from this aging playboy. I suspected that she was living vicariously through my shenanigans. After years of neglecting her own love life, between the stress of building her practice and lecturing at various universities, her only outlet was her clients.

After leaving her office one afternoon, I found myself exploring the neighbourhood. Her office was in the North End of Halifax, an area that was gradually gentrifying. Chic galleries and boutiques had cropped up along Agricola Street, amidst the old convenience stores and Mediterranean and Jamaican food stores. But there were still plenty of homeless people, most of whom were black, and I could tell by the way they looked at me they were none too pleased about the influx of newcomers to their home turf. But as I continued walking up and down side streets, not much seemed to have changed. The houses were still pretty rundown. I walked past a factory, the smokestack emitting a fine grey cloud. A bunch of women in uniforms walked through the parking lot, scarves wrapped around their heads like factory workers from another generation.

As I watched them lighting up, I was reminded of the chapter in which the Invisible Man ends up working at Liberty Paints. No sooner has he been hired than he finds himself caught in a union showdown, and everyone assumes that he's anti-union simply because this curmudgeonly black guy named Lucius Brockway has taken him under his wing. These scenes are the culmination of an even more bizarre sequence of events that find the Invisible Man stripped of his scholarship after giving someone influential a bad impression of his college. Narrowly escaping expulsion, the Invisible Man searches for work in New York, as he desperately tries to earn enough to cover the tuition for next year. But when he discovers that the letters of recommendation the headmaster gave him are actually a cruel joke, his prospects for employment suddenly contract and the full absurdity of his predicament hits him.

Where our narrator once saw himself as a rising star, he now struggles to hold a minimum-wage job, cut adrift in this strange city.

As I stared at the dirt-smeared bricks, his terror seeped into me. For I also needed to find a job – any job. It was becoming all too clear that my days at the university were numbered.

I met Katya by tearing a tab from the bottom of a page tacked on the board in the supermarket. What caught my eye were the Chinese characters in thick black ink. One of them looked like a stick woman, I thought at first. But the more I stood there, the more intricate it appeared, and I decided that it actually resembled a fat woman clapping her hands and swaying. Below the Chinese writing were words in English:

> *Do you suffer from mental conditions that leave you in a frenzy?*
> *Do you seek inner peace?*

Chi Kung can help

Expand your mind outward to infinity

Let the chaos of everyday life recede into nothingness. . . .

I didn't know much about Chi Kung, beyond having heard some talk-show host singing its praises. What was it? A new kind of yoga? It sounded pretty hokey, like some hippy-dippy cult, and yet something about the happy stick figure caught hold in my mind. I wanted inner peace. I wanted to connect with the universe. Besides, Harriet had said that I needed to make an effort to meet people, and this sounded a hell of a lot more interesting than Toast Masters.

Katya lived in a tiny white church just a ten-minute walk from my apartment in Halifax. The church was so small that it was hard to believe it had ever actually been a church.

Taped on the door was a slip of paper: "We mould clay into a pot, but it is the emptiness inside that makes it useful."

Bells jingled and the door opened on Katya's face. She was about fifty, a pale beautiful woman with wispy black hair and high cheekbones. She was wearing an ochre jacket cut like a kimono and black capri pants, which showed off a pair of fragile, bony feet. As she led me inside, my eyes were soothed by the scrolls covered in dripping black ink, reminding me of Granny's living room.

The chapel, which Katya called her "meditation room," was flooded with sunlight. A few people stood around in a circle, their feet also bare, arms hanging loosely at their sides.

"I literally couldn't – *couldn't* – get out of bed some mornings. Ever know the feeling?" a grey-haired woman was saying as we entered. "And now, look at me!" Her plum-painted lips veered up.

"Everyone, we have a new member," Katya said.

And this was how I began my path to enlightenment.

There was a robust South Asian woman dressed in a Puma sweatshirt standing beside the grey-haired lady, who had something wrong with her arm. It was stunted, shrivelled up like a chicken wing. The final member was a curly-haired guy whom I might have seen strumming a guitar outside Starbucks. A touch surly, a touch sad, they all had the air of strays. Joining their ranks made me feel like I'd just been admitted to an animal shelter.

"Imagine your head is hanging from a string," Katya said in a subdued monotone, barely moving her lips at all. This was how she always spoke during class. Sometimes, it seemed as if the voice didn't belong to anyone at all, as if it were coming down from some hidden sound system.

She was saying that our breathing gets messed up as soon as we leave the womb. We stop breathing naturally, from the belly, that zone of energy that comes from the umbilical cord. Our bodies are born filled with energy, but it remains blocked within us. We're born bursting with life, yet we grow old depleted of vitality, of *chi*. But if we can rediscover our *chi*, then our bodies will be harmonized, our relations with others will become serene, we'll all be part of a single universe.

Everything will be okay. Everything will *really* be okay. You'll have the energy to get out of bed in the morning.

"Pooooool. . . . Pooooosh. . . . " she slowly repeated over and over again, while making tiny waves with her arms. "Imagine the blue sky deeeeeep inside. . . . Imagine the sky all around you. . . . "

Outside of the meditation room, Katya's voice sounded completely different. She spoke rapidly with a slight twang, which I later discovered was Albertan.

"I knew from the start that we had this incredible connection," she said to me a few weeks later, after we'd become friends. "I could see the *chi* pouring from your eyes."

Perhaps if she'd had a daughter, rather than two sons and an ex-husband, her desire for female companionship wouldn't have been so intense.

Katya showed me a photo of herself standing beside Master Pong. After reading about him on the Internet, she'd travelled all the way to China. The master had done amazing things: cured people of cancer, bestowed sight on the blind, brought quadriplegics leaping to their feet. She'd studied with him for several months, at a monastery perched on a promontory overlooking the Yellow Sea.

The water was visible in the background, a frozen mist rising above her hair; she looked like a princess in a fairy tale. Her smile was mysterious, girlish, serene. Looking at the photo, I could feel the mist melting on my own skin, and I craved to experience that same feeling of beginning afresh.

Maybe I should head to the Yellow Sea and train to be a Chi Kung Mistress.

The first thing the Master had taught her was to stand like a tree. As Katya demonstrated this position over and over again, the aim of this exercise, she said, was to feel your toes descending so deep that they anchor you to the other side of the earth, the great life source of *chi*.

I closed my eyes and imagined my toes growing so long they penetrated straight through to that mysterious land of my ancestors. I waited for a moment of clarity, revelation.

I kept waiting. And waiting.

Every time I walked into class, my students looked at me a little more strangely. Where they used to sit scattered in the middle section of the auditorium, they were moving progressively further back and it upset me to hear my voice echoing into the empty seats.

"You can move closer – it won't do your grade any good to ostracize the professor," I was on the verge of saying. But somehow I doubted my attempt at humour would get a smile. They were more likely to just stare back at me, their eyes shining, like *Who is this freak?*

There was one student, a pudgy red-haired guy named Simon, who always sat alone at the front. His backpack was overflowing with books –

interesting, obscure books, like Robert Musil's *The Man without Qualities* and Kierkegaard's *The Concept of Irony*. Simon and I were getting to know each other, since he'd often shyly linger after class to talk. So I had some idea of what was on his mind. I knew that he didn't think much of the Frankfurt School and their negative dialectics, and I knew that the cool kids had been ostracizing him for some reason, unbeknownst to him, since first year. "Oh, I guess they find me arrogant or something," he said, smiling like he didn't even care.

He used to spend summers with his mother in London (London, *England*, he was careful to specify, just in case I thought he was talking about the bustling metropolis of London, Ontario). Ever since his parents had split up, his dad had been punishing him by sending him first to boarding school and now to this intellectual mecca. According to his dad, cities were full of drug addicts who were likely to lead poor Simon astray.

Sometimes, in the midst of lecturing, I would catch his eye and smile. *What are you doing here?* I wanted to shake him. *You should be at school in Montreal or New York, exploring the art scene, experimenting with your sexuality, falling in love, getting your heart broken.*

A group of my university colleagues invited me to Moonlight one night. It was Tony's birthday and the egg-drop soup was surprisingly decent for small-town Chinese food. But as we lingered over green tea and fortune cookies, I could tell something was on Karen's mind, as she stared at me over her tortoiseshell glasses. It was like I had a noodle stuck to my cheek.

"So you haven't applied for the position," she finally said.

"Oh, right." A month ago the department had released an ad for the contract position I currently held, which would be up soon. They must have assumed that I'd be eager to compete to jump on the hamster wheel for another year.

"I know you don't want to stay here forever," Karen continued, "but I would think you'd at least apply for it as a back-up, in case another school doesn't hire you this round."

I shook my head, a strange excitement in my veins. "I'm through with back-ups. I'm getting out of the profession."

Everyone looked stunned, as I explained that I was planning to move back to Toronto at the end of the school year.

"And what are you going to do there?" Karen's husband, John, asked, his eyes ironic.

I said that I might work for my uncle who had an architectural design firm.

"And what exactly will you be doing? Answering the phone?"

Karen kicked him under the table and signalled for the bill.

"Well, I have to say I admire your guts," Tony said.

Karen nodded. "If I were a few years younger, I'd probably do things differently."

"Oh, please." John rolled his eyes. He'd grown up on a farm and considered urban life highly overrated.

"It's just that. . . . " I struggled to be diplomatic. "I miss home. I miss my people."

"And who exactly are your people?" John asked.

I knew it was a lame thing to say. Yet it was true that after all these years of living a rootless existence, I longed to reconnect with a place, a people. I wanted to live amongst people who shared the same cosmopolitan outlook and came from backgrounds as diverse and complicated as my own.

"Oh, it's hard to explain." I reached for my coat.

"Poooosh. . . . Poooool. . . . Imagine the blue sky deep inside. . . . "

But my mind wasn't on a calm sky.

I was thinking about Ellison and his search to find himself as a writer, after studying and turning his back on music, photography and sculpture.

I was thinking about his assiduous efforts to learn from Hemingway, Joyce, Dostoyevsky and Malraux, reading their works late at night, while living in a barn in Ohio and hunting game to eke a living during the Depression. How desperate he must have felt back then. Had he ever doubted that his creative vision would see the light of day?

After we'd finished meditating, Katya said my hair was shining with *chi*.

Granny's condition was worsening by the day. Every time Daddy called it was to report that another body part had failed: she'd lost control of her bowels, her vision had gone pitch black, she'd stopped eating, stopped speaking. . . .

His days of making recordings and rehashing the past were over. Now he just wanted it to be over.

But panic swept over me when I thought about her slipping away. Had her grasping memories and half-disclosures all been for nothing? It was as though in compiling that photo album for Daddy and titling it "This Is Your Life," she'd been trying to communicate something important about her own life, yet the images remained nothing more than fragments of some elusive puzzle. There were so many things I still wanted to ask her. What had she wanted from life back in her youth? Why had she chosen to return from Japan on the eve of World War II, knowing she would be interned? How could she have stayed with Kaz all those years, after her own father had proven a lunatic, a sicko? And why did that twitch under her eye always act up whenever someone mentioned Kaz's death?

Maybe it was naïve of me to expect answers. Granny's life, after all, couldn't be read like a detective novel where all loose ends would be tied in tidy bows.

As I continued teaching *Invisible Man*, I found myself losing all critical distance and slipping into the world of the novel, as if the Invisible Man's odyssey to grasp his past somehow cast light on my own. In Ellison's surrealist world, reality dissolves into a bleak dreamscape where characters don't have clear motivations. Jim Trueblood appears as baffled and horrified by his desire for his daughter as we are. And we never find out why the Brotherhood withdraws its support from Harlem, after putting the Invisible Man in charge of the neighbourhood. The Brotherhood is this underground organization that recruits the Invisible Man ostensibly to join in their fight for equality across racial lines, but it soon becomes evident the organization is governed by hidden agendas, and as "brothers" start defecting and swinging to opposite extremes, the Invisible Man's world is thrown into chaos. No one is who he appears to be and allegiances shift with the wind.

The more I read, the more the novel got under my skin, and it especially creeped me out that the root of all the madness was an eccentric ancestor. What begins the Invisible Man's befuddlement is his grandfather's deathbed confession. A meek man who used to be a slave, he claims in his final breath to have been a traitor all his life and advises his grandson to continue the secret fight and "overcome 'em with yeses, undermine 'em with grins, agree 'em to death and destruction, let 'em swoller you till they vomit or bust wide open." After receiving this bizarre pep talk, how could anyone not be messed up?

I wondered if despite her appearance as the perfect Japanese doll, Granny harboured an equally duplicitous wish at the core of her being. Maybe that was why I could never see her with any clarity. Stripped of her identity as the jewel of the Japanese-American community and interned in the desert, she probably approached life from that point on as a haphazard nightmare, and like the Invisible Man's grandfather, learned to overcome 'em with yeses, undermine 'em with pretty smiles, marry a lunatic to get out of that god-awful camp, and agree with him to death and destruction.

Daddy had started reading *Invisible Man*, too. When he called one night, I decided to share my thoughts with him.

"Do you ever get the feeling in reading this novel that you've stepped into our family?"

"What do you mean?" Daddy asked.

"It's like we're all searching for some missing piece that will somehow make sense of our ancestry."

"Maybe," Daddy said slowly. "But it's more than just that. For all these years, I didn't even realize that any of this mattered. I was too busy working, travelling, making money. . . . My childhood was invisible."

I nodded. "That's how the Invisible Man tries to approach life, too. He keeps telling himself that his past doesn't matter, but the more he struggles to make it in a white man's world, the more his past keeps rearing its head, reminding him of everything he can't face."

Daddy fell into silence. I heard him flipping through the book. "In the end, the Invisible Man has to face the past. 'I yam what I yam!'"

I giggled. He was quoting the scene where the Invisible Man encounters an old black man selling yams on a street corner in Harlem. The buttery sweet smell makes his mouth water, but he's reluctant to indulge in the food that reminds him of his poor southern black origins. Throughout the novel, he craves chitterlings and pork chops as well, but can't eat them out in the open. Yet finally, the fragrance of the yams is simply too tempting and he's unable to resist his appetite for home. "I yam what I yam!" he jokes, assuming a new playful attitude in eating his past.

A sudden craving for Granny's *chawa mushi* overtook my stomach.

"Who knows but that, on the lower frequencies, I speak for you?"

I kept reading the last line of *Invisible Man* over and over again, and a hush came over me. I thought I might start crying.

Which would be embarrassing because I was at the Small & Tall Café right across from campus. Although the place was pretty empty right now, at any moment it would be swarmed by students.

Besides, I didn't have time for a meltdown. I was supposed to be drafting my brilliant lecture, which I was due to give in less than two hours.

But aside from a couple of bullets, my notebook was blank. It wasn't that I didn't know what I was supposed to say. To give a perfectly respectable lecture on *Invisible Man*, all I had to say were the very things that would make Ellison turn over in his grave. Funny how it's become fashionable to teach novels in just the way that would make the poor author retch. In his interviews and essays, Ellison talks at length about how in writing *Invisible Man*, he set out to write a novel that would transcend the vagaries of history and time. He didn't intend for his work to be read as a documentary of tough times in Harlem or a bootstrap tale about a talented southern black boy. Ellison had far greater aspirations in claiming his writing could speak to a universal audience, comprised of people of all colours. They might recognize something of their own triumphs and struggles in reading about the Invisible Man's tragicomic life – and such is the highest purpose of literature. To bring people together in shared wonder and delight.

It occurred to me that this is what I should have said when that student asked me what I meant by "unique interiority." Beyond skin colour and cultural differences, Ellison believed in the capacity of great literature to awaken a sense of common humanity, which makes us who we are as one-of-a-kind individuals.

But of course it would be too simple for my esteemed colleagues to take the author at face value on his vision. So the irony of all ironies is that while Ellison explicitly said his novel isn't about history, Professor X comes along and rips the text to shreds to show how Ellison didn't know what he was talking about – his novel is about nothing other than history. The race riot at the end of the novel looks ahead to the Civil Rights Movement, the Brotherhood can be read as an allegory for the Communist Party and its complex relationship to black worker struggles, blah, blah, blah. The most lyrical, poetic passages are reduced to nothing more than a history lesson in disguise. No doubt, these theoretical maneouvres allow the academic critic to show off how he or she knows so much more than the author – justifying the critic's dubious existence (for what, one might ask, if not undermining the author keeps the critic in business?). Yet the longer I stayed in this profession, the more cynical I became about the value of interpretation. Deep down, I was becoming convinced that the whole critical theory industry existed for no other reason than to allow a bunch of pompous academics to seek tenure.

For normal people, what does interpretation do except *kill* the very pleasures of reading? It isn't as if most fiction is so complex that it needs a guidebook to understand, or if it is complex, the complexity is a part of the whole mystical reading experience, and why would we want to demystify that? The more I thought about it, it made me ill knowing I'd almost signed my life away to destroy the very activity that had sustained me through the worst times of my life.

This being my state of mind, how was I supposed to puff out my chest and profess anything? What I actually wanted to do was break down in tears. That was the only response that felt honest and genuine at the end of the Invisible Man's final lyrical reflections on his retreat from the world to live in a cellar. Seeking to glean some lessons from his life, all he can come up with is that he needs time to hibernate away from other people's expectations. He's sick of playing the yes game, he's tired of pretending to be someone other than himself, and he's haunted to no end by his grandfather's dying words praising the art of seeming, not being. So what comes next? He has no idea. Living in his squat, he's simply passing his days and nights listening to Louis Armstrong tracks on an old record player he's managed to run on stolen power.

But through the darkness emerges a strange, ambivalent love of his past. For without all that crap to deal with, he wouldn't be who he is.

I dabbed at my eyes and let the waves of emotion wash over me, the final words of the novel ringing in my head. The novel actually gave me hope. I got the sense that the Invisible Man's period underground put him on the verge of some rebirth as a new kind of man, one who's more comfortable living with the complexities and contradictions of his own identity and past. And maybe that was what I'd been striving for all along, too.

When I looked up, a petite blonde was heading toward me. It was Vivian. She was wearing Lolita sunglasses and a mint-green nurse's uniform.

"Sorry about how I'm dressed." She sat down, like I'd been expecting her all along. "It's my day changing nappies at the home."

I smiled. "Want to swap jobs for the afternoon? You can deliver my lecture and I'll wipe asses. That seems like a fair trade."

"What? You don't love your job?" Her eyes widened. "I always thought you professors had it made."

"Oh, it has its ups and downs," I said vaguely, but who was I trying to kid? Now that I'd decided I was definitely leaving the profession, there was no reason for me to hold back. "Actually, I pretty much hate my job. I'm getting out at the end of the year."

"Oh my God, I totally understand – my life sucks, too." She leaned forward, like she was about to tell me a big secret. "You have no idea what's been going on out there."

"Out where?"

"At Clark's place."

It was true I'd been out of the loop. Bobby and I hadn't been seeing much of each other lately.

"Things are getting really tense," Vivian continued. "Jupiter's run out of money. He's stopped paying our rent. I think Clark's going to kick us out soon!" Helping herself to one of my napkins, she blew her nose.

Great. Now I had not only my own messed-up love life to deal with, but also this beautiful, snivelling little girl's.

My phone started buzzing and I could see from the call display it was Daddy. He'd left me a voicemail earlier, too. But how was I supposed to have time to chat when I was trying to write this damn lecture and getting sucked into playing shrink on the side?

"Have you considered seeking help from support services in the area?" I asked. "There must be organizations for single-mom teenagers, women's shelters, job search programmes. . . . "

She shook her head and started gnawing at her thumb. "Those kinds of people took my babies away."

"Oh. I'm sorry." The extent to which I was unqualified to play therapist weighed down on me.

My phone rang again. Why was Daddy so anxious to get in touch with me? I put it on vibrate.

"Well, if there's anything I can do. . . . Can I buy you a latte?"

"No, thanks." A smile played at the corners of her lips. "But I'd love it if you'd spot me a pack of smokes."

What a sucker I was. Her face lit up like a birthday cake as I passed over a ten-dollar bill. If only it took so little to make me happy.

After she'd scampered off to the convenience store, I noticed that Daddy had sent me a text message: *Granny dead. Funeral next week. Come home asap.*

chapter twelve

What, I wonder, was Uncle thinking those last few hours? Had the world turned upside down? Perhaps everything was reversing rapidly and he was tunnelling backwards top to bottom, his feet in an upstairs attic of humus and memory, his hands groping down through the cracks and walls to the damp cellar, to the water, down to the underground sea.

-Joy Kogawa, *Obasan*

The room where Granny's service was held had a long horizontal window, strategically positioned to show a strip of pale blue sky. Had the window been any lower, we would have seen a yellow bulldozer expanding the parking lot into the horizon.

The room was packed. I had no idea Granny had so many relatives and friends. But here they all were – row upon row stretching back; the funeral director had to get more chairs. I hoped they weren't here for the sushi afterward; Daddy hadn't ordered enough. Most of the faces I didn't even recognize, beyond a vague feeling of having looked up at them once at some event at the Japanese-Canadian Cultural Centre. And now I was looking down on their balding heads, their faces like wilted leaves.

It wasn't exactly shock or grief I was feeling; it was more like a vague greyness. All the blue skies in the world weren't going to purge the smoke clouds in my soul. The minister, a beaming ash-blonde woman, was full of generic words of comfort that might as well have been elevator music for all I cared. It infuriated me to think of her delivering the same Hallmark greeting cards three times a day.

Daddy, on the other hand, seemed strangely at peace. When he got up to read his eulogy, the lines of his face softened and his eyes shone with tears. His eulogy praised a woman who'd always loved animals and nature and had contributed tremendously to the Japanese community through her participation in women's groups.

He spoke of how much he would always treasure the final trip they'd made to Cape Cod so she could see the ocean one last time. On this trip, Daddy said, she opened up for the first time about how deeply she'd been affected by the internment, how shocked she'd been when the FBI agents came to take away her father in the middle of the night.

As Daddy spoke, my mind skipped back to his digital recordings, and it struck me as a tad absurd that his endless interrogations had smoothed out in his memory to a simple revelation of Granny's past. Still, I was glad he'd managed to drag the truth from her, if that was the reason for his tranquility.

"When we finally arrived at the ocean and walked along the boardwalk to the water," Daddy continued, "I asked Mom what she liked about coming to the sea and she said, 'When I was a little girl, I liked the sound of the waves and the salty smell.' This struck me as sad, because at this stage in her Parkinson's, she wasn't able to smell the salt air. But then, she said that the look of the ocean was always changing and renewing its appearance and she liked that sense of change. At that moment, I understood why Mom continued to seek new opportunities and changes throughout her life, and was always able to cope in the most difficult times."

An image of Granny staring out over the dancing waves pierced my mind, and I imagined that the salty sting in my own eyes was the sea air she could no longer smell. More images of her stirred in my brain – her hands folded like the wings of a dove around a steaming cup, the way her face would quietly beam as she contemplated the placement of a flower in her *ikebana* arrangement. A year ago, I would have never believed that Daddy would be capable of triggering these emotions. But all our months of reading together had paid off in opening him up emotionally, honing his powers of observation and self-reflection, enriching his ability to feel things more fully.

A look of pure grief came over his face, as he tried to elaborate on the difficult times Granny had faced. "In the early 1970s, after Kaz's death, things were hard for all of us. . . . " His eyes misted over and he gripped the podium.

For the first time ever, I saw my father cry.

I wiped at my own eyes with the back of my sleeve, fearing that I might have to step up to the podium and read the rest of the eulogy for him. I felt strangely protective of my father, like our natural roles of parent and child had been reversed, and it pained me that the day would come when he would become as helpless and vulnerable as Granny.

Wide-eyed looks were shooting around the room, and a few people coughed. But it was more than just Daddy's tears that made people uncomfortable. I'd never understood what it was about Kaz's death that still seemed to fill everyone with such dread.

Daddy managed to wrap up with a few nice words and Ted got up. I was hardly even listening to his reminiscences about all the places they'd travelled – I was too nervous about having to get up next. I was supposed to read a poem. I'd chosen Dorothy Livesay's "Green Rain," a poem about a girl remembering the feathery green fringe on her grandmother's shawl. It's a beautiful poem, twinged with nostalgia and filial regret, but it didn't begin to capture the tragedy and bafflement I still felt upon reflecting on Granny's life.

To be honest, I didn't want to read a poem at all; I would have preferred to read from Joy Kogawa's *Obasan*. While packing to come back, I'd thrown the novel in my suitcase on a whim – a little internment literature to lighten my mood – and I'd been reading it ever since.

I'd forgotten how much I loved this novel about a schoolmarm seeking to understand her Japanese immigrant past. After receiving word of her uncle's death, Naomi Nakane returns to Lethbridge, Alberta, where she was raised by her uncle and aunt (Obasan) after the family was released from the internment camp. The mystery of how Naomi's mother disappeared during the war – she visited Japan to care for an ailing grandmother and never returned – drives the story. It echoed the mysterious absence in my own grandmother's life after her mother took up with the businessman in Japan.

Absent mothers, vanishing motherlands. Would any of us ever understand our pasts?

A sudden urge to surprise everyone seized my stomach. Fishing the novel from my shoulder bag, I began flipping through it. Maybe I wouldn't read the poem at all. Which part of the novel could I read instead?

There's the part where Naomi reflects on being haunted by the loss of her mother: "Just a glimpse of a worn-out patchwork quilt and the old question comes thudding out of the night again like a giant moth. Why did mother not return? After all these years, I find myself wondering, but with the dullness of expecting no response."

Or there's the section where we learn the secret that Naomi was sexually abused as a child: "His name is Old Man Gower. He lives next door. I can see his house beyond the peach tree from my bedroom window. His belly is large and soft. His hair is thin and brown and the top of his head is a shiny skin cap. When he lifts me up in his arms, I smell something dank and unpleasant."

And then, if you still have the stomach for it, there are the painstaking descriptions of the exhibition grounds where the Japanese-Canadians were first deported: "The whole place is impregnated with the smell of ancient manure. Every other day it's swept with chloride of lime or something but you can't disguise horse smells, cow, sheep, pig, rabbit, and goat smells. And is it dusty! The toilets are just a sheet-metal trough and up till now they didn't have partitions or seats."

I wondered what response I would get from my family if I were to read these passages, a montage of Granny's life. Shocked stares? A shower of tears? The painful thaw of memories flooding back? It would be glorious to jar everyone from their superficial calm, the contrived sadness of funeral decorum.

But when my turn came, I decided to be a good girl. I got up and read the poem.

At the tea afterward, Aunt Wendy was running around greeting people, while Daddy just stood by the wall, looking distant and calm. Where was his anger, where was his burning resentment? It was as though these feelings had suddenly vanished along with the life sucked through the soles of Granny's feet.

As I stood there watching my father, Aunt Tetsuko sidled up. I could feel her heavy presence beside me, a black rustle, a flash of silver. I pretended to be staring at the wall where old photos were being projected from Daddy's laptop and she started looking at them, too, so after a while I really was immersed in them: the photo of Granny after just giving birth; the one of her playing with Daddy in the snow; a shot of her in a white sundress standing outside their shabby apartment in Verdun. More pictures of her were displayed in black photo albums, laid out behind the table of sushi and sweets.

To the end, I found myself fascinated by the sheen of Granny's smile, the electric sparks flying from her eyes. There appeared nothing disingenuous about that smile, and yet how could I believe its magazine-perfect gloss, knowing what she'd endured?

The image flipped, and I stood there in its midst, immersed in a stream of hollow light.

The next photo was a family portrait. There was Kaz beaming alongside Granny, his arm behind her, cradling the small of her back, while Aunt Wendy, a newborn swaddled in white, curled against her breast. They looked like the perfect 1950s family – father powerful, mother beautiful – except for one little glitch. My father looked surly. As he sat in front of Kaz, he looked like he wanted nothing more than to squirm away, like he couldn't stand having his father's hand on his shoulder. So much for the "perfect family" charade.

I felt Aunt Tetsuko edging closer to me, the layers of her shawl crinkling.

"Why did Granny come back from Japan to marry that lunatic?" I said.

Aunt Tetsuko said nothing.

And then I wasn't sure whether I'd said anything at all (maybe the thought had just whizzed through my head).

"That lunatic was my brother," she said at last. "My favourite brother. I still remember when he was a teenager, he'd come home past his curfew and our father would lock him out. He had to sleep in the shed. I wanted to take him a blanket or something, but then I'd get in trouble, too."

"I'm sorry. But you know what I mean."

"Don't idealize Japan," Aunt Tetsuko said. "If Masako had stayed there, who knows what would have happened to her?"

An image of Naomi's mother at the end of *Obasan* flashed before my eyes. At last, we learn the horrible truth about why she never returned from Japan. She never came back because the atomic bomb dropped. Nagasaki went up in a white flash, the flattened flames running along the ground. The blood and pus, the flies and maggots. The visible horror burned into everyone's skin.

"Your grandmother was too shrewd for that – she knew how to save herself. She knew that with Kaz wrapped around her baby finger, our father wouldn't let her languish in the camp for long."

Daddy was lingering at the end of the table, and his ears perked up. "That's not true. Mom came back from Japan because she was in love with Kaz."

It surprised me to see on my father's face the stunned look of a little boy who still yearned to believe that something beautiful had been there in the beginning. I didn't understand where this flash of optimism was coming from, I'd become so used to Daddy's cynical ways. It was fascinating and moving to see his mother's death release him, freeing him to let go of the old wounds and unanswered questions.

And now all that was left was a child's bewilderment.

"All I'm saying," Aunt Tetsuko continued, "is that it wasn't all Kaz's fault. Masako had a hand in making him crazy with her grand expectations – all she ever wanted was to be Mrs. Doctor Somebody. If he'd married a different kind of woman, his life could have turned out very different."

"You mean he wouldn't have killed himself," Daddy said flatly.

Aunt Tetsuko's jaw trembled and my own knees went jittery and I wasn't sure whether I'd only imagined what he had said, in a perverse twist of my writerly imagination. But the truth was too familiar and dark, as if, in a way, I'd known it in my gut all along, and had only been waiting for it to come into focus all these years. Since childhood, I'd always been aware there was something weird about how Mommy averted her gaze and Daddy rolled his eyes whenever Granny mentioned my grandfather had died of a stroke. "Pass the rice, please." "Seen any movies lately?" For there was no euphemism pretty enough to take the edge off what Kaz had done. So the family had played along with Granny and her desperate need to keep up appearances – fearing her own fragile sanity might go crashing over the edge.

I didn't feel shock at the fact of Kaz's suicide so much as shock at hearing

Daddy talk openly about it.

"How did Kaz kill himself?" I asked, breathless.

Aunt Tetsuko blanched.

"He hung himself in the basement," Daddy said softly. "I was the one who discovered his body hanging from the rafters."

The basement. The house on St. Clarens. Within seconds, an image formed in my mind, like a Polaroid coming into focus, working its horrible magic. The sooty pane sinking into the ground. That hot, cavernous space. Suddenly it made sense why my father refused to get too close. While I had been staring in the basement window, he'd stood back a bit, drawing circles in the mud with his toes.

I didn't know what to say, so I stared out the window at the parking lot, trying to focus on the yellow bulldozer, poised to break the concrete. Behind me, relatives were chatting in Japanese and English, happy as picnic-goers at a family reunion. Someone dropped a glass with a shatter; there was a lot of fuss. As my eyes welled, the yellow object wavered and dissolved into a splotch that didn't really resemble anything.

"Pooool. . . . Poooosh. . . . Feel the blue sky deep inside. . . . "

I stood in my old bedroom doing the exercises Katya had taught me, her voice echoing in my head. But I couldn't clear my mind. I couldn't see the clear blue sky. All I could think about was death and a great black void.

What goes through a person's mind in the moments leading up to death? Like the narrator of *Obasan*, I was haunted by this question. I supposed it must vary depending on a person's disposition. In Granny's case, her last thoughts were probably of the ocean. She had the instinct for self-preservation to cling to her happiest moments at times of stress. The salt air, the ever-changing waves – these memories must have lulled and comforted her, blotting out the dark times.

No, it wasn't Granny I was worried about. But Kaz haunted my dreams.

Suicide was an entirely different order of death. Misery and despair must have seeped through his entire body, overpowering all rational thought, outrunning nature, a rapidly expanding spill of black paint. Ruined. Sullied. Shit everywhere. He must have sunk to a depth of darkness where no memories were visible, because with memory – no matter how bad it might be – there's always the possibility of a happier memory latching on, restoring that fragile thread connecting you to the human race.

So it was all over now. I knew the horrible truth about why Daddy, Granny and none of the Shimos could sleep. I knew the fate of my grandfather, whom Uncle Haruki had said I resembled, tears glimmering even as he looked away. It was over. Yet I couldn't bear to let it just be over. I couldn't bear to go back to the university like everything was fine. I wanted *more* of . . . something. More self-understanding, more insight, more empathy. More of whatever elusive tranquility now graced my father's cheeks.

I delayed my flight back for a few days, emailing my colleagues and students that I was suffering a time of grief. *Grief.* Suicide had to be the ultimate grief. A point at which you truly believed your feet were never going to touch the sandy bottom, and there was no hope of ever coming up.

Woolf, Hemingway, Yukio Mishima, David Foster Wallace. . . . How many other great writers had taken their own lives?

I thought about Hemingway's bullfighting scenes and how the artistry of the sport lies in its proximity to death. What makes Romero so skilled as a bullfighter is how closely and calmly he lets the horns pass each time, never overemphasizing the turns of his cape to create the illusion of danger. The danger is real and he revels in its nearness – perhaps this was the allure of suicide for Hemingway. A flight of pure daring and artistry in the face of death. To control, to make artful. Suicide was perhaps a way of extending the beautiful control that a writer exerts over the world of his novel to his own life, right to the end. For endings were important. It didn't make for a nice narrative arc to have the hero go out as a mass of smelly, decaying flesh, a shit-laden diaper.

For Woolf, on the other hand, suicide appeared to be an act of love. *I know that I am spoiling your life, that without me you could work. . . . What I want to say is I owe all the happiness of my life to you,* her suicide note to Leonard read. Killing herself was a way of saving her beloved from the darkest aspects of herself. Her final act of walking into the river was an attempt to communicate something beautiful. "Death communicates," as she'd written in *Mrs. Dalloway*, following Septimus Smith's luminous flight through the window. Death communicates: love. Or at least, in the lover's manic mind.

I wondered if Kaz had left a suicide note. I wondered if his state of mind had been at all similar to my favourite authors' as they courted death. But I sensed in my gut that the reality of his last moments were probably much quieter. Pervaded by a damp grey terror.

The truth was there was no way of knowing what had gone through Kaz's mind, as he stood on the stool playing with the rope. It was beyond the powers of my imagination.

For the next few days, I wandered around the city wearing a ridiculously light jacket, relishing the late November cold. I was hoping I'd get sick with pneumonia. An excuse to skip giving my exams.

I ran into my old friend Clara Kim, on a street corner close to where her parents lived, and I was so immersed in my own turmoil that she had to grab me by the arm before I recognized her. We went for coffee at a new place where the coffee was served in steaming beer mugs.

"I'm sorry to hear about your grandmother," she said, when I told her why I was in town.

"Thanks. She was old and ill, so we expected it."

Clara fidgeted with a packet of sugar; my flip answer had made her uncomfortable. "God, I could really use a cigarette."

Things with Jim weren't as great as they'd once been, she said uneasily. She was taking a long trip to India to think things over. And besides, there was a lot to be learned from healing practices in India, all of which would be useful when she opened her naturopathy clinic, but I got the sense that she was really looking for a way to heal herself. When I pressed her about what was going on, she looked away and said she didn't want to go into it. But the dark circles under her eyes made me think her marriage was in serious trouble.

"Call or email me anytime," I said, suddenly overwhelmed by guilt that I'd envied her, that I'd assumed she had the perfect marriage, the perfect life.

My oldest friend, and I hadn't been aware that she, too, had been suffering all this time.

After we parted, I walked to the subway. On impulse, I got off at Ossington and kept walking west, my heels turning to ice cubes, but of course my direction wasn't entirely random – I was heading toward the house on St. Clarens. Like a crazed detective revisiting the scene of the crime, I examined the peeling paint and bottles and cans in the recycling bin, sniffing this and that. I went around to the backyard, ignoring the "Beware of Dog" sign, and peered through the murky glass into the basement. I stood there for a long time, as if I were waiting for a film to begin: an opening shot of Kaz drinking whiskey and strumming his guitar, his brow knit, a man tormented by demons. . . . I wanted to suck meaning from the house, as if its decrepit remains held clues to my ancestry and my future.

But in the end, the house was just a house. Foundation crumbling, eavestrough falling off.

Mindlessly, I walked along Lansdowne and ended up in a bar lit like a laundromat. The place was virtually empty aside from an old man watching *The Price Is Right*. I ordered a beer and read a bit of *Obasan*, letting the scenes of illness and death wash over me:

"Daddy is sick, Nomi."

"When will he come home?"

"Maybe never."

"Is he going to die?"

Death and homesickness loom everywhere in the novel. In many ways, it's an elegy to a people – my people – who thought they'd be given a fair shake in Canada, only to have their dreams nipped in the bud. I recalled reading an interview of Joy Kogawa where she talked about how the novel was intensely autobiographical; like Naomi, she was evacuated from Vancouver as a young child and sent to a camp at Slocan, and later made to work on a beet farm under the government's dispersal strategy. The scenes of dislocation and loss mark the death of a community and culture, forever left flailing to recover something of its original self. Written as a spur to action, *Obasan* gained prominence in the 1980s as Japanese-Canadian and Japanese-American communities lobbied their governments for redress. With mixed results. ($20,000 per internee was a drop in the bucket compared to what had been originally lost, according to my other grandmother. She used to reminisce about her father's chain of restaurants and big white house with a tennis court – everything had been auctioned off at bargain-basement prices. The more she chuckled and reminisced, the grander the house became, and eventually it had not only a tennis court, but also a rabbit hutch and swimming pool out back).

Memories of home. A lost childhood. Not surprisingly, the most moving passages of *Obasan* speak to all those things that can never be redressed.

But as I continued reading and searching for insight, Kaz's life remained as fuzzy as ever. No doubt, he'd suffered a terrible blow to his ego during the war years, but he hadn't suffered nearly as much as others in the community, due to his privileged position as the doctor's son. And yet, while his friends and relatives had rebuilt their lives in the decades after the war, and even achieved some degree of prosperity and happiness, Kaz had remained mired in his dark mood. Whatever love or obsession he initially felt for Granny turned warped, violent. His was a different order of death drive and it made my skin crawl to think that I might take after him. But what could I do?

The albums Daddy had prepared for Granny's funeral were stacked on the dining room table. Some of the photos I was already familiar with, but others were new. Aunt Wendy or Aunt Tetsuko must have provided them.

A picture of a house caught my attention. It followed a sequence of photos of the house on St. Clarens, but this house was different. The door was freshly painted and the bricks looked so new they almost looked fake. The fancy railing along the steps and neatly clipped hedges out front gave the house a forced air of luxury. Daddy, in his late teens, stood on the lawn smiling distantly, while Aunt Wendy played on the lawn.

"Daddy, where was this picture taken?"

He looked up from his book. "Oh, that's the house on Greenmount Court. That's where we moved after St. Clarens."

I'd never contemplated another house. "Why did you move there?"

"Kaz never liked the Lansdowne area – he said it was full of junkies and hookers. He kept complaining so his mother finally sold the house and gave him most of the proceeds, I think. Kaz bought this other house out in Etobicoke, as far away from the riffraff as possible."

"Was he happier there?"

Daddy's face stiffened. "No. Almost as soon as we moved, Kaz suffered a stroke. By that point, he was really losing his mind."

A hush came over my stomach, and I pictured Kaz in bathrobe and slippers, his skin ashen, his body partly paralyzed, limping around the house, an old man before his time. So this was where he'd reached the end of the line – here was the basement where he'd hanged himself. It was strange to think that the picture-perfect suburbs had been his deathbed, the very place he thought offered refuge from the grime.

"Do you want to see the house?" Daddy asked.

I nodded and jumped up, surprised.

On Prince Edward Drive, the traffic was surprisingly heavy. Everyone was slowing down to get a glimpse of an accident at the intersection. I played with the radio trying to find the jazz station, but finally gave up.

"I've been enjoying reading *Obasan*," Daddy said.

"I suppose it covers a lot of historical stuff you already know."

He shook his head. "Reading the novel, I'm learning a lot about our history. Joy Kogawa's about ten years older than me, so she actually has memories of the camp. I was born after the internment, and since my parents never talked about it – no one did – it was as though the whole thing had never happened. I had no idea of the internment for the longest time, and even when I began to ask questions I still never got a clear picture of what had happened. Of course I was aware of the racism against Japanese-Canadians, but that just seemed a fact of life."

I stared out the window at the crushed metal and flashing lights. A paramedic was transporting a woman on a stretcher, and for a moment I almost wished I were outside amidst the din. It would have been easier to take than this horrible awkwardness that had come over me now that my father was finally opening up.

"I guess that's why it was so important for you to get Granny to talk," I said at last.

Daddy nodded. "All my life, there was so much I'd never understood."

We turned onto a street lined with tall trees and large lawns surrounding each perfectly beautiful, perfectly uniform house. The suburbs, a place of forgetting.

But just when Kaz thought he was home free, the bitterness and depression closed in.

Daddy pulled into a cul-de-sac and parked in front of a large grey bungalow. Every surface was freshly painted in various shades of grey, a tasteful, muted palate. Two SUVs were parked in the driveway, boxes from Price Club visible inside.

"They've completely changed it," Daddy said, standing back. "The door used to be yellow and the front was brick."

"Can we go around the back?"

"No, these people probably have a house alarm."

"Maybe they'll be nice and invite us inside."

"I wouldn't want to go inside. I never liked this house as much as St. Clarens, even before Kaz killed himself."

He said it so calmly, yet beneath his air of not caring was a tremor of something else, a twitch, a wounded animal. Everything looked blurry through my tears, and I felt more tongue-tied than ever.

"It's funny how even though Kaz finally got what he wanted in moving out here," Daddy continued, "he still couldn't be happy. Out here, he was more miserable than ever."

"Why did he kill himself?" I asked.

Daddy said nothing. A slight ringing filled my head.

"He was just one of those people who could never be happy. He felt that life had screwed him at every turn."

I gasped and waves of grief hit my chest. I stared at the freshly paved driveway, a river of tar.

"Maybe I'm also one of those people."

Daddy looked at me hard. "Listen, Leslie, you're the only one who can make yourself happy. So don't do anything to please me. I gave up on all that bullshit long ago – *become a doctor, carry on the family tradition, make the family proud*. Believing that crap pushed Kaz over the edge. Your only responsibility is to make yourself happy, so if you're miserable as a professor, get out."

I nodded, everything bright and blurry.

"But don't expect someone else to figure things out for you," he said. "You have to find that thing that drives you."

It was the first time Daddy had ever said I was free to pursue my passion.

I pictured him standing all alone on the flying field, gazing up at the sky, his model airplane turning figure eights, and it amazed me what he'd come through in order to find his passion. Considering the horrors he'd lived through, he might have resigned himself to a life of turmoil and depression, but instead he'd pulled himself through. He'd broken with Kaz's dark legacy.

For the first time in a very long time, I felt hopeful about my future.

"Where's Kaz buried?" I asked.

"Around the corner," Daddy said.

"Can we go there?"

Kaz's grave was under a large tree that might have been lush during the summer. The first snowfall had left a fine white powder in the letters etched into the marble: SHIMOTAKAHARA.

When I voiced my surprise at how new the headstone appeared, Daddy said Granny had replaced it a few years back, after teenagers had vandalized the cemetery.

"When was the last time you were here?" I asked.

"Not since Kaz's burial."

But he told me that Granny used to visit the grave several times a year. Granny had shown Daddy photos of the grave ornamented with flower arrangements in the summer; she'd always saved her best *ikebana* for Kaz.

His eyes were shining with amazement as he told me this. And I shared in his wonder at my grandmother's capacity for forgiveness and forgetting.

chapter thirteen

Words such as *love, passion, duty,* are so continually used they grow to have no meaning – except as coins or weapons. Hard language softens. I never knew what my father felt of these "things." My loss was that I never spoke to him as an adult. Was he locked in the ceremony of being a "father"?

-Michael Ondaatje, *Running in the Family*

A year later, I was sitting at my desk in my new apartment. I looked out at the curlicue B of the Hudson's Bay Company lighting up the sky, counterposed to the full moon, the jagged dip of office towers filling in the background. In the foreground, a small park lined with spindly trees and graffiti-covered benches gave all the homeless people a place to congregate. For the past twenty minutes, I'd been watching an old man rifling through his shopping bag, doing an inventory of his worldly possessions.

The view was by far the best thing about the apartment.

The floor in my kitchenette was covered in dingy tiles that were impossible to scrub clean and the bathroom was so small the door barely closed. The elevator didn't work and the narrow corridor reeked of takeout.

But at least I was back in Toronto.

And don't get me wrong, I was happy about that. But I'd been less than thrilled to be ousted from my childhood home by whom else but Daddy?

A pile of unpacked boxes were stacked in the corner, where Daddy had left them when he helped me move in yesterday.

"Do you want us to help you unpack?" Mommy had asked. "Do you want me to sew curtains?"

"*No*, just leave everything," I said. "You've done enough. You wanted me out of your hair, didn't you?"

"You heard her," Daddy said. "She wants to be alone."

So we'd parted on a sour note, which had been souring for a while. When I'd moved back to Toronto last May, my parents had agreed I could live at home until I got back on my feet. Of course Daddy had wanted to know how long that would take, so I'd said a year. He didn't look thrilled and I certainly didn't relish the thought of being infantilized, but I was exhausted.

The move back had sapped me, physically and emotionally. Since I couldn't afford to ship my stuff back, I'd had to drag a lot of stuff to Value Village. My favourite skillet, an antique lamp. But the worst was dealing with my beloved books. It caught me off guard when I suddenly found myself tearing up as I was packing up my office at the university – the very day I thought I'd been looking forward to with gleeful anticipation. But waves of sorrow came over me as I took my books off the bookshelves, one by one, and placed them in two old suitcases that I was selling to a used book company. Afterward, standing in the doorway of my empty office, I'd felt like a doe-eyed undergrad who'd just finished her B.A. and had cleaned out her dorm room. Except I wasn't a twenty-two-year-old ingénue; I was a thirty-year-old ex prof. Overeducated, but underskilled. Floundering without a profession.

So I'd resigned myself to sleeping in my childhood bedroom, while I endured the stress of answering job ads and rewriting my academic CV as a resume (what employer would care about a stellar paper I'd given at the

Edith Wharton Society?) and then the stress of going to interviews and simply waiting to hear back.

To my amazement, however, it didn't take long to find employment. By the end of my first month of looking, I was more gainfully employed than I'd ever been in academia. Ellen Powell, my dear old boss, came through for me. She offered me a communications position at her NGO. I began working with international development consultants to draft project proposals and give presentations about the capacity-building work the organization was doing in countries across Africa and the Americas. The work was interesting and I was good at it. The only drawback was it was a contract position. I was crossing my fingers that Ellen would be able to convince the CEO to make my job permanent.

So life was looking up. But I still felt off-kilter. Although I'd accomplished a lot, I had this gnawing hunger in my gut, but I had no idea what I was craving. It made me edgy and probably not the most charming person to live with. And Daddy was his usual edgy self, sprawling out on the sofa so there was nowhere for anyone else to sit. It didn't take long for us to start going at it – arguments, tears, and sometimes full-on blowouts.

"When are you going to start looking for your own place?" he'd ask every morning over breakfast.

"I don't know." I stared into my cereal bowl.

The truth was that much as my parents were driving me crazy, it was nice having someone to come home to. It was nice having two retired parents who spent a good deal of the day tending to the comforts of home – vacuuming, cooking elaborate dinners. Homemade pad thai was Daddy's latest experiment. After years of living alone, subsisting on sandwiches and takeout, I was ready to be well nourished for a change.

I guess you could say I was regressing.

The flipside of having retired parents is that they also have time to peruse the classifieds. One day, I came home from work and Mommy was smiling nervously.

"Your father and I found you the perfect apartment," she said.

"But I'm not ready to move out!"

Daddy's arms were crossed. "It's time, Leslie."

After my father kicked me out, I actually began to feel better. My mind felt clear, like an empty closet. For the first time in a very long time, I felt alone with my own thoughts – freed of gossiping students, far away from the resentments of childhood.

Every evening I stood in my new bedroom, my arms hanging loose by my sides. After a while, I let my arms float to the ceiling, arcing over my head, my hands slowly descending over my face, my neck, my chest, my abdomen. I imagined a light waterfall passing over the front of my body, purifying my skin, as Katya had instructed me. All of a sudden, it no longer seemed quite so hokey. A warm energy actually seemed to be emanating from my palms and cool tingles were washing all over me, leaving me feeling cleansed, refreshed.

It wasn't like I expected my future to be nothing but calm blue skies, but for the first time in a very long time I felt that everything might actually be okay.

As I walked to work, the winter air smelled pure, intoxicating.

The best thing about my new job was that it involved writing. While some of the writing was tedious and bureaucratic, most of it was rather interesting. As part of our marketing strategy, I'd been asked to write a series of human interest stories for the newsletter about the unintended results of what our consultants had accomplished overseas. Doctors from Quebec had discovered that old medical equipment no longer in use at their own hospital could do a world of good in Mali. A consultant from Vancouver ended up adopting a little boy in Ghana, whom she met while idling in traffic on a street corner. It amazed me the lengths people would go to to connect with others and share their lives.

These stories caught hold in my imagination, and I began writing about them not only for our newsletter. In the evenings, bits and pieces surfaced in my mind in different form, as I reclined on the sofa and let my thoughts wander. . . . I began writing fragments of first-person narratives in my notebook, trying to see the world from my characters' perspectives.

It was a delicious return to the way I'd written back in grade school.

The way I read was changing, too. Now that I was freed from constantly thinking about my next lecture, all those distorting "isms" that had formed a lens through which I'd seen everything were falling away, blissfully falling away. And I was left feeling like a kid, seeing the world as just a smoosh of colours, shapes, sounds. I loved being able to focus on the words themselves, awash in all their mystery and beauty.

Often, I flipped through interviews with well-known writers. I was intrigued by how in his *Paris Review* interview, Ted Hughes discusses the way he always writes everything out in longhand because the shape of his own handwriting takes on a life of its own and sparks sudden, unexpected meanings. I loved Joyce Carol Oates' reflections on how she'd always felt her parents' memories were her own memories: it was as though everything that had happened to them had happened to her. The past was like Daddy's photo album, where every picture might open up into a scene and the feelings and emotions imbuing each character were at once my own and not my own. Sketches of things that had happened to Daddy and Granny took shape in my notebook, as I slipped into their heads and imagined myself breathing the musty air of St. Clarens one moment, the salty sting of the ocean the next. They belonged to me. All their memories belonged to me. Our past was there for my imagination to create anew.

I'd also developed a penchant for memoir, particularly memoir of a more creative bent. "How I have used them. . . . They knit the story together, each memory a wild thread in the sarong," writes Michael Ondaatje in *Running in the Family*. For years, I'd been meaning to read this epic memoir, which tells the story of his return to his childhood home in Ceylon (now Sri Lanka).

Tingles ran all over my back as I read about the ghosts of his ancestors looming larger than life. Each conversation he has with his half-deaf and half-blind relatives serves as a thread tying him back into the tapestry of his family history: the stories about his eccentric grandmother, Lalla, who became legendary for serving a live goat for dinner, the endless rumours surrounding his father's madness and drinking and suicide attempts – most famously by walking naked down a train tunnel. I wondered if Kaz had ever been so reckless, so desperate. All these stories come into focus as Ondaatje weaves them into the story of his own origins.

How I longed to travel back, too. I wanted to gain access to that well of family myths and collective memories of which I'd only scratched the surface. So I was yearning to go back – back to Vancouver, Kaslo, Portland, Japan, wherever. Simply *back*.

After months of not hearing from Josh, I got a phone call one evening.

"Wow, I can't believe you actually did it," he said, after I told him I was back in Toronto. "Most people just talk about quitting, while resigning themselves to a life of misery."

"Well, my sanity was at stake."

After an awkward pause, he said, "Guess what? I'm quitting my job, too."

"Really?"

Josh paused, enjoying the sense of suspense.

"So what are you going to do with yourself?" I asked. "Back to chef school?"

He chuckled and rattled off the name of some big investment firm I'd never heard of. As it turned out, he wasn't quitting being a lawyer at all. He was leaving his current position to take a higher-powered position as VP legal at an investment firm. No, he hadn't seen the end of his eighteen-hour work days.

"Congrats," I said and really meant it.

It was funny how his maneouvres and attempts to get under my skin no longer had the same effect. Maybe I'd always think of him as the road not taken, but my old wistfulness had transformed into a kind of relief, or acceptance of fate – everything happens for a reason. No doubt, he was an eccentric, arrogant, hilariously funny guy who'd left his mark on my youthful self. But I no longer thought of him as the guy I was meant for. It was exhausting to be around him, even for a brief phone call.

"So let me ask you," he said, "am I going to be a character in one of your books?"

Not surprisingly, things with Grant also fell apart. What had once struck me as mischievous, roguish behaviour – dirty text messages, kinky love letters – lost all allure once he lived two subway stops away. We met a few times for after-work martinis and sometimes it even led to a tussle at his place, but the excitement had fizzled. It irritated me how he kept checking his iPhone. (His girlfriend kept trying to track him down and for the first time, I actually felt guilty). All our old rituals of seduction failed to excite me. When he commented on how I seemed less energetic than usual, I had to tell him our arrangement was no longer working. Of course he tried to convince me otherwise, but we both knew things were over.

"Call me if you ever change your mind," he said, leaning back against the dented pillow. "You never know, you might want me the next time you feel depressed."

"Thanks, but I'm not planning on another career crisis for at least two decades."

"You were a lot more fun when you were a wreck."

"We'll always have Antigonowhere." I kissed him on the cheek, and that was the last time I ever saw him.

I began reconnecting with old friends and going to parties, where I met Phillipe. He was a finance director in the healthcare industry and we dated for a few months. He was sweet and articulate and French (read: sexy), but in the end we just didn't have enough in common. His idea of a good weekend was to play squash and soccer and then go for a long run, even in pouring rain, while I wanted nothing more than to curl up with my notebook. Still, we parted as friends, and a month later I heard he was dating an equally athletic banker.

When Oliver and Nicholas emailed me that they were having a party, I wasn't sure I was up for it. I hadn't seen them since Tania took me to their party last summer, and she wouldn't be going to this one since she'd recently moved to Switzerland. But Saturday night rolled around, and there I was sitting at my desk staring out the window. I was supposed to be getting out and expanding my social circle – all that single-girl-in-the-city stuff. So I put on a slinky black dress and hopped in a taxi.

The loft was packed by the time I got there. Palms sweaty, I looked around for the hosts or at least a familiar face from the last party.

Oliver was at the sink cleaning oysters, and he gave me a big hug (being careful not to touch my dress). He said Tania had told him to get me out more often. The kitchen was crowded with wine bottles and glasses and the claustrophobia was just starting to close in on me, when I caught sight of Chris leaning against the counter.

"Hello, you." I went over.

He greeted me with a warm embrace and I caught a hint of a subtly spicy cologne emanating from beneath the collar of his crisp black shirt.

As he poured me a glass of wine, I said, "I know something we can toast to. I've moved back to Toronto."

His eyes lit up. "Welcome back."

I smiled and the wine continued flowing, as we chatted about Mies and Le Corbusier and Deleuze and Benjamin before I finally got up the nerve to tease him about pulling a disappearing act at the last party.

"Sorry about that," he said. "When I went down to find my friend, he was having a rough time – his girlfriend had just broken up with him. I came up about twenty minutes later, but I guess you'd left by then."

I could tell by the way Chris was looking at me – shyly, wistfully – that he wished we'd talked longer.

"So what are you reading these days?" he asked. "I trust that an ex-lit prof still reads a lot."

I told him about *Running in the Family*.

"I remember reading that book," he said. "I love what Ondaatje does with collective memory."

We began talking about how all families are probably haunted by ancestral ghosts and I started to tell him – somewhat drunkenly – about all the things I'd discovered about my own family over the past two years. My grandmother's ruined childhood, my grandfather's suicide, the internment – I just kept talking. And then, suddenly a bit abashed, I started intellectualizing a little, referencing Freud's concept of the uncanny, which he seemed perfectly familiar with (or else he was very good at faking it). The conversation brought back the heady memories of grad school, except now I was talking with a stylish architect dressed in all black, rather than a bearded would-be Thoreauvian.

Just as I was starting to fade, Chris brought up the topic of his own family back in China. Before the Cultural Revolution, his grandfather had had two wives, and both wings of the family had lived unharmoniously under one roof, leading to all kinds of scheming and machinations.

But it was late, and the room was slowly spinning. "Sounds fascinating. I've got to hear more about this when I'm not so tipsy."

"Let's have coffee some time," he said.

I smiled and gave him my number.

One afternoon, I was in my parents' neighbourhood visiting my dentist. On a whim, I dropped my copy of *Running in the Family* through their mail slot. No note, no envelope with Daddy's name on it, nothing. But I hoped he would read it.

At the core of the memoir is the story of a son's belated search for his father. Ondaatje wasn't around during his father's decline and dementia, the alcohol level in his blood rising ever higher. He wasn't there when his father died from a brain haemorrhage. By that point, his parents had long been divorced and Ondaatje and his siblings were scattered around the world. So the first time he went back was the day of his father's funeral, and there's a heaviness to his conscience as he now returns again to search for vestiges of the man he never really knew. Through a montage of interviews with those who were closest to his father in his final days, we learn of a man devoted to his animals – he raised a flock of chickens that could rival any in the region, and a pack of dogs for each of whom he made up lovely songs – and all the small, gentle gestures of his life begin to come into focus. His care for others. The ever-expanding darkness in his brain. His innocent, childlike pleasure at small things, even as his behaviour became increasingly cryptic and bizarre.

I felt it was important for my father to read this, since he hadn't been there for his father's decline. *Your father got out of the house, he saved himself, he vanished. . . .* Aunt Wendy's bitter words echoed in my head.

I wanted him to know it wasn't too late. It wasn't too late for us to travel back in time and recover the past, unfurling its mysteries, fleshing out the bare skeleton of the father he'd never known. For I, too, felt a gnawing absence in my gut, the void of a missing ancestor. I wanted to commune with Kaz, with all my dead loved ones. I wanted to get to know them, if only in my imagination.

Chris and I had coffee, followed by dinner at a little bistro overlooking the park in Yorkville. We talked for hours about a hodgepodge of things: our favourite libraries around the world, our favourite houses, and we even fantasized about designing a house centred around a wall of books, ladders sliding back and forth along the lofty cathedral ceiling.

By the time we got to dessert, he was telling me about a courtyard house in Guangzhou that had been in his family for generations. He wanted to modernize it, reinterpreting its typology, while respecting the memories attached to every stone. It was the house where his father had hidden during the Second World War.

Excitement fluttered across my chest.

"I don't usually talk this much," he said suddenly.

"Me neither."

"How did I get onto this topic?"

"We've just been digressing all evening, going from one extended footnote to the next."

"Extended footnotes." He smiled.

We had several more coffees and dinners – leaping from one footnote to the next – and before long we were hopelessly in love. I knew I could talk to him forever and the conversation would always intrigue me. And he called *me* his muse.

Eight months later, we moved in together, renting a bright, airy house on the Ossington strip. All the prior drama in my love life melted away and I'd never been happier or more content.

As time passed, my relationship with Daddy gradually got better. When his birthday rolled around, I took him to a jazz concert, followed by dinner, just the two of us.

We went to a pasta bar that had just opened around the corner from where Chris and I lived. The place was packed because it had gotten rave reviews in *NOW* and *Toronto Life*. Steaming plates of tagliatelle with goat ragout floated by and Daddy eyed the food hungrily.

"It's funny how this area's become the hip place to live," he said. "Growing up around here, I never thought I'd see the day."

Daddy tore at a piece of bread. I was struck by a new gentleness to all his gestures, verging on hesitancy, as though he didn't know what to do with his hands. And nor did I. It was as if we didn't know how to behave around each other anymore. Now that my life was going so well, he'd been relieved of his patriarchal duty, and while I knew he was proud of me, it left us in uncharted territory. Neither of us was quite sure of our new roles, so we just smiled at each other, like on a bad first date. We sopped bits of bread in olive oil. He asked me about how work was going and I said I was happy my position had been made permanent. I told some funny stories about my colleagues.

Finally, I asked if he'd read *Running in the Family*.

"Oh, yes." He smiled. "Thanks for slipping that through the door. I enjoyed it. And I can see why it made you think of me."

I wondered what he'd been thinking as he read the pages that chronicle the decline of Ondaatje's parents' marriage – his mother waking up and contemplating divorce, after years of standing by her husband's antics. Walking down a three-quarter-mile long tunnel carrying a set of clothes for her naked husband went beyond the call of wifely duty. "She followed him and coped with him for fourteen years, surrounding his behaviour like a tough and demure breeze." That line stood out in my mind and made me think of Granny. Had Daddy had the same thought, too? Had he thought back to the train trip to Portland they'd made all those years ago, just the two of them, when he was a little boy? I imagined elk and bison and all the other animals Granny had promised they'd see through the train window dancing before his eyes, as he speculated about how different their lives could have been had she chosen to stay in Oregon. Had she chosen to leave Kaz.